The *Kung Fu* Book of Caine

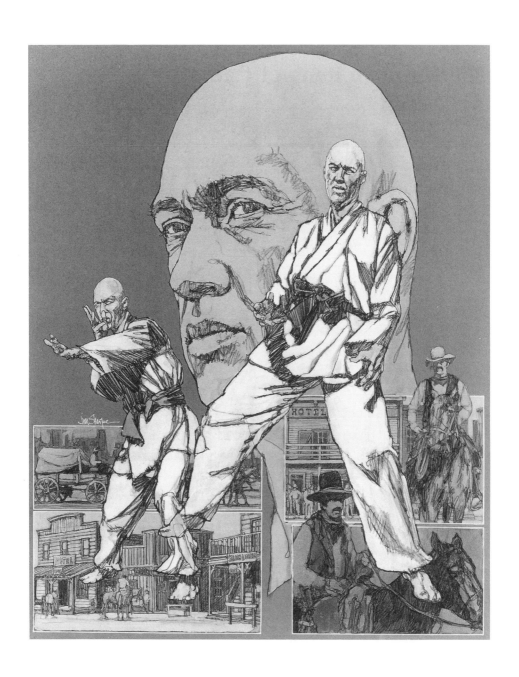

The *Kung Fu* Book of Caine

The Complete Guide to TV's First Mystical Eastern Western

HERBIE J PILATO

CHARLES E. TUTTLE COMPANY, INC.
Boston   Rutland, Vermont   Tokyo

PUBLISHED BY CHARLES E. TUTTLE CO., INC.
of Rutland, Vermont, and Tokyo, Japan, with editorial offices at 77 Central Street at McKinley
Square, Boston, Massachusetts, 02109

Library of Congress Cataloging-in-Publication Data

Pilato, Herbie J.
    The "Kung fu" Book of Caine : exploring television's most mystical eastern western
drama / by Herbie J. Pilato : foreword by David Carradine.
        p.   cm.
    ISBN 0-8048-1826-6 : $16.95
    1. Kung Fu (Television program)
PN1992.77.K78P54   1993
791.45'72--dc20   93-11307
                                                                                CIP
Production: Editorial Inc.
Cover & text design by Judy Arisman, Arisman Design
Sumi-e by Kaji Aso
Production manager: David Emblidge
Editorial development: Debra Spark
Composition by Editorial Inc. The text of this book is set in Trump Medieval.

Credits and acknowledgments: Every effort has been made to obtain appropriate permissions and
to credit copyright holders. Rights holders who wish to contact the publisher should
communicate with the editorial offices of Charles E. Tuttle Company, Inc., 77 Central Street,
Boston, MA 02109

All information in this book has been checked by the author and publisher against scripts and
other source material provided by Warner Bros. We regret any errors in biographical data that
may have been caused by the unavailability of relevant documentation.

First Edition

10 9 8 7 6 5 4 3 2 1

Printed in the United States of America

To the unity of all religions, churches, temples, monasteries,
and spiritual centers of light and good beliefs. May they help us to
seek and embody wisdom and understanding above all things.

Contents

Foreword by David Carradine   ix

Preface   xiii

Acknowledgments   xv

Part One THE MAKING OF *KUNG FU*

Chapter One: The Appeal of Grasshopper   3

Chapter Two: Creations   13

Chapter Three: The Shaolin Way   19

Chapter Four: Kwai Chang Caine   27

Chapter Five: Masters and Other Supporting Characters   39

Chapter Six: Behind the Scenes   47

Part Two THE STORIES OF *KUNG FU*

Introduction: A Guide to the Movie Pilot and the Original Series   57

Chapter Seven: First Season Episodes   65

Chapter Eight: Second Season Episodes   93

Chapter Nine: Third Season Episodes   125

Chapter Ten: The Return of Caine   153

Chapter Eleven: The Legend Continues   163

Appendixes

Selected Biographies   171

Emmy Nominations and Awards   184

Sample Shooting Schedule   186

Index   193

Illustration Credits   203

Foreword

A long time ago, way back in the prehistoric seventies—December, 1971, to be exact—a bunch of us started shooting a movie for TV called *Kung Fu*. We had no idea of what it would lead to; we just thought it was a really great script. Because of my background and because of some of my innate and acquired abilities, I found myself in the center of what would become an international phenomenon.

We all just went to work and did the best we could. The rest of it was up to the public, and, I guess, the era we were in.

As we worked, the whole thing began to grow, all by itself. We did our best to keep up. Eventually, it became a THING on the planet, completely out of control. We had a tiger by the tail; no one could tell us what we were supposed to do next. We were breaking fresh ground; dealing with the great unknown.

Our basic concerns to make this show what it was were absolute authenticity, historical accuracy, the chronicling of the troubles the Chinese immigrants experienced in America, a hint of the need for social revolution, lots of Chinese philosophy, caring for all life, a lot of heart, and superior technical quality in the films, in the writing and in our execution of all this.

Somewhere right in the center was this character, "KWAI CHANG CAINE" or "LITTLE GRASSHOPPER" who bound it all together. It was his sweetness and his strength and the special kind of humor that went with him that kept people tuning in every week. That was my job. Trying to find what was going on in this character's mind was something that possessed me and eventually obsessed me. I always thought it all had to be perfect and if it wasn't perfect, it was up to me to make it that way, somehow.

The whole thing flashed by so fast (we were only on the air for three years), it was sort of remarkable we made such a large impression. When I left the series, February 5th, 1975, I thought we had done our work. I went on to a feature film career and left "LITTLE GRASS-HOPPER" behind.

As the years passed, the series, miraculously I thought, actually grew in popularity during reruns. Many times someone would say to me, someone perhaps on the street or in a restaurant or at a party, "Are you ever going to do any more of those again?" One day I said to myself, "Well, I guess I have to; apparently our work was not finished." The martial arts explosion which the series caused is still running rampant across the big and little screens, not to mention in the Dojos and Kung Fu academies. Very little of any of this explosion had much to do with the philosophical points we were trying to make.

I tried to put back together the original bunch, but they were spread so far afield—retired, or passed on, or just too busy with other projects, but I kept trying, and somehow with a lot of help and a lot of new guys, we now have the whole thing back together again. The format is different but the message is the same. I hope this time people will get the point. It's not a question of kicking and punching; it's a question of trying to see the world in a good light. I've always thought someone should give a try at chronicling the original series—what the stories were about, who was involved, the great actors (to some of whom we gave their early opportunities: Harrison Ford, Robert Duvall, Don Johnson, Keith and Robert Carradine, and many more)— but mainly to give a clear account of exactly what it was we did.

During the series I tried to give some indications of the correct chronology, the most obvious of which being that I began the series with a shaved head and I grew my hair, never cutting it, until the series ended, when I shaved my head again; so that it is possible when viewing any one show to know exactly where it appears in the 62 segments, simply by looking at my hair.

When I heard of Bruce Lee's death, I changed the color of my shirt from brown to saffron, another attempt to pinpoint the moment. When we changed the KUNG FU advisor to a real Shaolin Master, thereby plunging into some of the real secrets and eschewing the more theatrical and less authentic KUNG FU fighting, I arranged to lose my hat; so if you see me without a hat, you know that it is the real thing. When I actually began formally studying KUNG FU (I know it's probably hard to believe everything that went before was done the way dance choreography would be done, but that's the truth of it), I arranged to have my entire costume trashed as a result of being buried under an avalanche (a segment I directed myself). Subsequently I came upon another renegade Shaolin Priest who gave me a set of the traditional black silk KUNG FU garb which I wore for the rest of the series.

Very early in the series I took off my shoes and carried them over my shoulder. I did this because in pretending to kick someone, every once in a while I missed and hit the guy; and with my big farmer shoes on, that would hurt. As everybody knows, on TV, we try not to actually hit each other; it's all supposed to be just pretend.

Another way you can tell when a particular segment of the series was shot is by the progression of the flutes. Sometime during the first year, I began carrying a bamboo flute over my shoulder. The first flute was a very small one. The second flute was somewhat longer with a bend in the middle. The third was a full-length flute which I actually made on camera during one of the segments. That one was destroyed during the avalanche. The fourth flute was a little tiny one made for me by Jose Feliciano and Cannonball Adderley.

I think it's a great idea someone has decided to take the trouble to try to put down for historical purposes a complete picture of what we did back then. I just hope he gets it right.

The new series, *Kung Fu, The Legend Continues*, carries on all the traditions of the old series, with some new stuff. We have to deal with modern times, situations that all of us face every day; but through it all, CAINE walks unchanged.

I guess five years or so from now we'll have to come up with another book . . . . . . count on it.

David Carradine
Sun Valley Ranch

Above: *Behind the cameras of the original* Kung Fu *movie pilot with David Carradine* (at left) *and David Chow, the show's technical adviser.* Right: *In front of the cameras with Carradine as Caine and Chow as the renegade monk in the series' pilot.*

Preface

When I was a small couch potato sprouting up in Rochester, New York, the adult world would clamor, "Now, Herbie J, don't sit too close to the TV set, it's not good for you." Well, maybe it wasn't good for them, but it was fantastic for me. One might even say it was a mystical experience.

For as long as I can remember, I, like Kwai Chang Caine of *Kung Fu*, have been on a spiritual journey. I was born into a traditional Italian family and raised a Catholic. In my twenties, I informally excommunicated myself from the church and began to search for something else. I studied Asian philosophies and Eastern religions, read from a variety of books, and looked into an assortment of practices, including astrology, numerology, the study of reincarnation, and lexigramology. (Part of the latter involves finding the hidden meanings in names. For example, "Caine" may be found in the name David Carradine.)

As a result of all I learned, I eventually rejoined the Catholic church with a new peace. I realized that I am supposed to be a Catholic (this time around!). I recognized that we all share a common humanity and that individuals, when joined together, can become instruments of peace, beacons of light. We can be examples of faith, compassion, generosity, forgiveness, health, and happiness wherever we go. Just like the character of Caine. He always possessed a strong respect for others. He never forced his ideas upon others. He taught by example, without the intent of teaching. I know that I have learned a lot from the *Kung Fu* series—a lot about integrity, style, and grace. I know, too, that, with this book, my life has come full circle, because I have had the opportunity to combine my spiritual exploration with my belief that television can be educational.

The ninety-minute movie pilot for the *Kung Fu* TV series premiered on the ABC network on February 22, 1972, and drew a 33 percent share of the market. *Kung Fu*, which began its three-season run as an hour-long dramatic series the following fall, was an Eastern western, a western with a twist, because it was set in the West and in China. It showed the ethos of the American West during the mid- to late 1800s, and it presented Asian philosophy and esoteric thought to TV viewers. On June 28, 1975, the last episode of the original series was aired. At the time, the show was near the top of the ratings. In syndication, it remains popular. *Kung Fu: The Legend Continues* is a new weekly hit that now airs in 225 markets.

This book provides background for viewers of the new series and for aficionados of the old one. I start by talking about what made the show so popular, and then look back at how the series came into being. Later chapters address the principal characters and the actors who played them, while others examine the art of *kung-fu* as depicted in the series and provide behind-the-scenes information about the show. The movie pilot and all sixty-two episodes of the original series are individually described and commented on. Additional material about the *Kung Fu* sequels (first aired in the 1980s) and the new series is provided as well. The appendixes offer biographies of the stars and other information.

To write this book, I conducted interviews in the summer of 1992 with the writers, directors, actors, and producers of the program. Warner Bros. contributed scripts and synopses of the various shows, and I drew liberally from this material. All quotations are from the Warner Bros. scripts, or from my phone interviews with *Kung Fu* cast and crew. Ultimately, this book was created to pay homage to an atypical series, to profile an esoteric yet popular TV show that has been extremely important to me. My hope is that readers will derive, at least, a fraction of the enjoyment from *The* Kung Fu *Book of Caine* that I have from the series.

Herbie J Pilato
Rochester

Acknowledgments

Many people helped me gather the information for this book. Cast and crew of Kung Fu—the old series, the new series, and the sequels—made themselves available for interviews. Specifically, my thanks go to David Carradine, Gail Carradine, Radames Pera, Ed Spielman, Howard Friedlander, John Furia, Jr., Herman Miller, Alex Beaton, Harvey Frand, Guy Lee, Ralph Ahn, James Hong, Soon-Teck Oh, Robert Ito, Beulah Quo, Mako, David Chow, Dr. Kam Yuen, Michael Greene, Robert Schlitt, Richard Lang, Durrell Royce Crays, John Badham, Marcela Cardinale, Elinor Karpf, Jason Karpf, and Jerry Thorpe.

People at Warner Bros., the Association of Asian/Pacific American Artists, the University of Wyoming, *TV Guide*, and elsewhere helped me gather scripts, photographs, and miscellaneous information for this book. Special thanks to the following people at Warner Bros.: Sheryl Haft, Eileen Hazo, Michelle Sucillon, Kris Smith, Grace Ressler, Patty Feldman, Lenny Bart, Milton Segal, Laura Sharpe, Greg Mayday, Ellen Gonzales, Louis Mahinay, Thelma Howard, and Rusty Mintz. Also, special thanks to Professor Neil Kubler, Chinese Department, Williams College. Thanks, too, to Bill Yih for his time.

Charles E. Tuttle Company, Inc., and Editorial Inc. helped me realize my dream of producing this book. And many people, dead and living, have inspired me in this project and others. To God, my friends, my family, and my teachers—loved ones all—I give my thanks.

*Courage,
cowardice.
These are but
words of an
orphaned
moment. Think
only of the goal of
your beginning.
Be neither brave
nor afraid, but at
Peace.*

MASTER KAN
*Episode #5,
"The Soul Is the
Warrior"*

Part One

THE MAKING OF *KUNG FU*

I don't think that anyone who ever had anything to do with the series will ever forget the surreal feeling . . . on the Kung Fu *set. You would walk onto the studio lot, through the huge gates at Warner Bros. . . . and almost magically became a part of the world of* Kung Fu.

JAMES HONG
Kung Fu *guest actor*

*Young
"Grasshopper"
Caine (played by
Radames Pera)*

CHAPTER ONE

The Appeal of Grasshopper

THE SINGLE WORD "grasshopper" has served, for many years, as an informal tag line for the *Kung Fu* TV series. Almost everyone who has any enthusiasm for the show remembers the scene in which the word was first spoken: Caine, a young disciple of the art of *kung-fu*, is at a Shaolin temple in China. He is with his mentor, the blind Master Po (played by the late Keye Luke), and it is clear Caine feels sorry for Po, sorry that the old man has lost his vision. Po responds to the pity by showing Caine that blindness hardly diminishes certain men.

MASTER PO: Close your eyes. What do you hear?
YOUNG CAINE: I hear the water. I hear a bird.
MASTER PO: Do you hear your own heartbeat?
YOUNG CAINE: No....
MASTER PO: Do you hear the grasshopper which is at your feet?

The boy opens his eyes, looks down at the ground, and sees a grasshopper.

YOUNG CAINE: Old man, how is it that you hear these things?
MASTER PO: Young man, how is it that you do not?

From then on, Young Caine's nickname is Grasshopper, and the signature line of the TV show is "Grasshopper" or "Snatch the pebble from my hand." The latter line refers to a scene involving

Caine and his other principal teacher, Master Kan (played by the late Philip Ahn). Master Kan is the Senior Reverend and Grand Master of Martial Arts at the Shaolin temple. He is an imposing figure, and yet, one senses kindness in him. In the famous scene, Kan is interviewing Caine for acceptance into the temple. Kan never formally admits the boy. Instead, he points to a pebble that lies in his open palm, and he says to Caine, "As quickly as you can . . . snatch the pebble from my hand." Caine tries, but Kan's hand closes before Caine can get to the pebble. Then, Kan says to Caine, "When you can take the pebble from my hand, it will be time for you to leave."

By the mid-1970s, the word "grasshopper" and the phrase "Snatch the pebble from my hand" were as familiar as "I can't believe I ate the whole thing" and "EE-dith" have been to other TV audiences. Of the word "grasshopper," Ed Spielman, who wrote the original *Kung Fu* script with Howard Friedlander, says: "I have written numerous screenplays, books, and articles, and numerous films have been produced of my work. But out of everything I have ever been associated with professionally . . . I'll be remembered as the guy who created Grasshopper." The explanation for the popularity of the word seems to be that, unlike the catchphrase from the Alka-Seltzer commercial or the cry from Archie Bunker, the signature line from *Kung Fu* is not about overindulgence or anger or any of the mundane emotions and sensations we associate with the rest of popular culture. It's a line about spirituality and, as such, it's a line that points to what was, for many people, most impressive about the series: its ability to popularize the ineffable; its ability to translate Eastern philosophy into a Western medium; its ability to function so well as a "Chinese western." As David Carradine, star of the series, once pointed out to an industry official, the *Kung Fu* show was that most unusual of things, a commercial television series about a man trying to atone for his sins.

"We had a good story, maybe a great story," David Carradine says in trying to explain why the series was so popular. "And one of the things that I figured out for myself was that the story was not about truth, it was about love." His coworkers tend both to agree and to feel that the very message of the story was something the public was longing for. That said, the story was designed in a significantly clever way so that it could sustain the sort of philosophical questioning that came to define it.

The show's essential dilemma was presented in the *Kung Fu* pilot (originally aired in 1972 and initially titled *Kung Fu: The Way of the Tiger, The Sign of the Dragon*). The story goes as follows: An orphan appears at the gates of the Shaolin temple. His name is Caine and he is of mixed lineage. His father was American, his mother Chinese. Although only "pure" Chinese have been admitted to the temple in the past, Caine distinguishes himself, so the head of the temple, Master Kan, accepts him. Caine stays at the temple till his early manhood. During those years, he disciplines his mind and his body. He learns about the major *kung-fu* systems, the Animal styles that teach a person how to manifest physically the disciplines of grace, self-control, speed, patience, and so on. He learns how to walk so softly that he can walk over rice paper without tearing it. He learns how to develop his *chi*, his inner strength, as well as his outer strength.

At length, Caine is ready to leave the temple. He is able to snatch the pebble out of his master's hand. Before he departs, Caine must walk down a long pathway till he reaches an urn full of hot coals. On one side of the urn is a dragon; on the other side, a tiger. The various masters with whom Caine has studied stand to the sides of the urn. He takes his leave of them. Caine has a great deal of affection for Master Po and this good-bye is a particularly difficult one. Then, Caine presses his arms to the side of the red-hot urn and lifts. He is branding himself with the mark of the tiger and the dragon. The brands signify that Caine is no longer a mere disciple. He is a Shaolin priest. This is a rare distinction, and when people who know what it means meet him in later life, they will, invariably, be awed.

Some years after Caine leaves the temple, he meets Master Po near the Temple of Heaven in the Forbidden City. It has long been Master Po's ambition to attend a festival here during the Full Moon of May. Po once confessed this to Caine when Caine was still his student. The confession had been an intimate one, since a Shaolin is not supposed to have ambition. Still, Caine remembers the ambition and goes to the festival in the hopes that he will see his old friend. They meet and talk. Then, they are jostled on the road by the Imperial guards and the arrogant nephew of the Imperial House. An altercation ensues, and the nephew draws a pistol and shoots and kills Po. Caine hurls a spear at the nephew, immediately killing him. Then Caine cradles his friend until he dies.

Caine is ashamed of his action. Everything Po has taught him suggests that he should not have killed the nephew. He apologizes to Po, and Po, as he is dying, forgives him. Still, Po is worried for his friend. It is no small thing to have killed the nephew of the Imperial Emperor. Po warns Caine, "There will be a price on your head. . . . You must leave the country."

Po gives Caine his sack, containing all his worldly belongings, and then dies. Caine flees China for the American West. Presumably he means to hide in all that open space. In the pilot for *Kung Fu*, and in subsequent episodes, the essential conflict is set up. In America, Caine will always have to deal with two threats: the threat from those from China who are hunting for him in his adopted country and the threat from the racist, greedy people he encounters there. Frequently, these two threats will converge when an American learns that there is a $10,000 reward for capturing Caine.

In the pilot, the threat from China is represented by a Shaolin monk gone bad. He comes after Caine to get the reward money. Such an objective is totally inappropriate for a Shaolin monk, as Caine's character makes clear in the following scene when he realizes why the monk is after him:

CAINE: For money? A Shaolin monk does not sell himself like a handful of rice!
YOUNG MONK: A man can tire of begging. You are *more* than a handful of rice.

In the pilot, the American threat is represented by corrupt railroad men who are willing to threaten the lives of the Chinese laborers if, by doing so, they can save money.

As he deals with the threat from China and the challenges in America, Caine has to come to terms with how he has acted in the past, and he has to discover how he should act in the future. Thus, as David Carradine aptly points out, in some ways, the *Kung Fu* story is the oldest of human stories. Carradine explains: "The story of *Kung Fu* is actually the story of Cain, the first murderer, in the land of Nod, east of Eden, who carries a mark upon him placed there by God. And his conflict is to resolve himself about killing his brother. . . . *That's* why his name is Caine."

Interestingly enough, the choice of the name Caine for the main character was entirely accidental. Still, Friedlander and Spielman, cowriters of the pilot, admire Carradine's ingenious interpretation; certainly the reading fits with their own sense of the story.

Part, then, of the series' popularity had to do with the narrative appeal of the show. The overall premise was clever, and the episodes' individual stories were intriguing. Beyond that, the program's actors, writers, and directors suggest, what made *Kung Fu* special was its general sensibility, its spirituality, its timeliness, and, on a more mundane level, its visual appeal and its style.

In broad outlines, *Kung Fu* was a story about love overcoming hate, good triumphing over evil. As such, it preached nonviolence and thoughtfulness. In each episode, the question of action (versus nonaction) was a significant one. Each week, Caine struggled with the oldest of human questions: What does it mean to be a man? What does it mean to be a good man? How should one act?

As Radames Pera, who played the young Caine, points out, these questions were not necessarily unusual for television, but they were explored in a context that was new to TV viewers. "I mean, wherever did a television viewer have the chance to see someone—a TV character—practicing Zen philosophy or Taoism on a national medium?" asks Pera. "It was just unheard of."

In fact, the spirituality that writer Spielman incorporated in the pilot was Asian, but not only Asian. "I tried to combine universal spiritual elements," Spielman explains. "I employed that which was closest to me, Jewish thought, and a whole lot more."

Despite the presumed universality of the philosophy, the story had to play itself out in a particular setting, and that setting was northern China and western America. That, too, seemed to appeal to viewers. American audiences had always been receptive to

westerns. In addition, says David Carradine, audiences of the early
seventies were increasingly curious about the wisdom or inner
peace that Asian philosophy offered.

Michael Greene, who appeared in two episodes of the series,
expands on this thought when he says the show's initial appeal had
to do with "a subliminal inner need." He observes that "people
were really ready for something like *Kung Fu*. It came at a time
right after the sixties and the mind-expansion experiments that
were so popular. . . . [Then] here comes this television series that
kind of took everything to the next step."

The style echoed the philosophical direction of the series and
was an additional part of the show's appeal. John Furia, Jr.—who
served, at various times, as writer, story editor, and producer for
the show—explains: "The whole show displayed a lack of the
frantic, frenetic motion for its own sake that I think is part of the
American culture and a lot of the American media. Our characters
moved and spoke slowly and tersely. They used fewer words rather
than more. They didn't repress their emotions; they controlled
them, as well as their actions." Nonetheless, Furia says, the characters weren't statues; they were human, and *that*, he concludes, is
why audiences, particularly young audiences, were so drawn to the
show.

James Hong, an actor who appeared in the *Kung Fu* pilot and as
a guest star on the series, echoes this point. He says that the program "offered a slower pace than life itself. It kind of eased and
relaxed you as you would watch it. And it simultaneously offered
words of wisdom to digest in the process—something that people
could incorporate into their own lives."

In addition to all this, the series employed some engaging visual effects and narrative devices, all of which added to the "look"
of the show and, probably, its popularity. To tell the story, as
Kung Fu enthusiasts well know, the creators relied on flashbacks.
Flashbacks allowed the viewer an entrée into Caine's memory, a
way to leave the western United States and travel to the Shaolin
temple in China. There, viewers saw what Caine saw: the significant parts of his past, his life as a disciple at the temple. Thus, the
viewer could learn two things: (1) how Shaolin priests were

trained, and (2) how Caine was able to incorporate essentially abstract teachings into the concrete, often problematic situations he encountered in the West.

Richard Lang, who directed several episodes of the series and was assistant director of the pilot, credits Jerry Thorpe, original producer and director of the show, with pioneering ". . . the 'look' and the 'feel' of *Kung Fu*. It was Jerry who started the visuals with the candles, . . . the slow motion, forced perspective, and long-lens rack focus techniques. The rest of us, certainly awe-inspired, tried our best to add to and increase the visual impact."

The slow motion that Lang refers to was used for action scenes. Although people have suggested various reasons for why the scenes were done in slow motion (for example, to undercut the violence on the screen), the real reason for the decision was, according to John Furia, style. It was not, he insists, because of some censorship of the script that required the violence to be toned down. Rather, Jerry Thorpe introduced the balletlike visuals because they were "in keeping with the entire philosophy of the show," says Furia. "The slow motion also added to the totally different 'look' that we were seeking to attain. It was wildly different, we thought, for a western."

The original show's associate producer, Alex Beaton, says the slow motion came about when the initial screenplay (*Kung Fu* was originally intended to be a full-length motion picture) became a TV movie. At that time, he explains, those working on the project "realized that David [Carradine] could move like a ballet dancer, and we knew we had the perfect opportunity to utilize those talents to give the severely rapid, occasionally lethal-looking self-defense scenes a lighter touch."

Carradine says the slow motion was indeed used in an effort to get certain images past the Federal Communications Commission, but it created as many problems as it solved; for while it may have made the scenes seem, on a certain level, less violent, it also lengthened them.

On a very practical level, there is one more explanation for the use of slow motion: it helped the viewer see what was going on. For instance, when a weapon was thrown through the air, the audience simply couldn't see it unless the film was slowed down.

Kung Fu spin-off products include a lunch box with a matching thermos.

It's true that in American minds kung-fu, as well as the series *Kung Fu*, is associated with violence. Clearly that association was part of the popularity of the show—even though that association was antithetical to the mood of the program. Still, writers' and producers' motives aside, certain people were tuning in for the fights. The apparent paradox arises because there is an aspect of self-defense to the martial art of kung-fu, and, therefore, self-defense was part of the series. However, to reduce the martial art to fighting is to miss the whole point of the discipline. Indeed, if you ask regular students of kung-fu how many times they have been in a fight, they will usually say, "Once," or "Never." After all, kung-fu is not about being a warrior but about training the mind and body.

Still, as viewers of the series know, there was a fight in each of the *Kung Fu* shows. Furia explains this seeming contradiction by saying, "I was very insistent that we show violence." The show was set in the West, during the 1800s. This was, Furia points out, "a violent time and place, and when Caine did become physical and use his ability to defend himself and/or others, they always had to be in dangerous situations. There would never be a case where he would act violently simply because his ego was bruised

 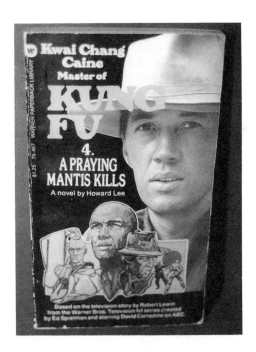

Two of the several Kung Fu *novels that were released in the 1970s*

or someone challenged him. And we were always sure to show that violent acts were painful and ugly," Furia adds. "You know when a person was hit by one of those lightning-fast moves of Caine's . . . , we would show that it was very painful. And we tried to make it as realistic as possible. If an evil character was hit by a blow that was disabling, then he would be disabled. One thing that I did not want to do was glorify violence and have people reveling in violence in a show that was preaching nonviolence. I thought that would be hypocritical."

Ed Spielman points out that the show was not really a show about violence. It was a show about the *reaction* to violence, about "appropriate action and reaction, the ability to deal with conflict." When young Caine asks his master what the most appropriate way to deal with an attacking force is, his master tells him, "Run away." This, his master says, is the "simple and preferred method" for the man who prizes peace over victory. It was the essential lesson of the series: peace is more important than victory, nonviolence is to be preferred to violence. And, it turns out, it was a lesson audiences were eager to hear and rehear.

Kwai Chang Caine
(David Carradine)
works on the
railroad in the
Kung Fu pilot.

CHAPTER TWO

Creations

T HE STORY of the *Kung Fu* TV series starts in Brooklyn, New York, with Ed Spielman. As a teenager, Spielman loved Japanese cinema, especially the work of Akira Kurosawa. Spielman also studied martial arts, but his interest didn't deepen until he began to study radio and television production at Brooklyn College. At that time, he had a friend who was a martial arts instructor. One day, the friend mentioned that his wife—who happened to be Chinese—could "flatten" him with one or two fingers. Spielman was intrigued. He asked his friend what his wife's training was, and he said, "*Kung-fu.*" Spielman started to research the subject, and he began to study Chinese. At the time, he didn't have any clear plan about what he was going to do with the information. He was just interested.

Meanwhile, Spielman was trying to work, with his dear friend Howard Friedlander, as a comedy writer. The vocation, however, didn't get in the way of Spielman's avocation. He was actively pursuing his interest in the Far East. Says Friedlander: "I think he really believed at one time that he was the reincarnate of either a Samurai warrior or some mystical Chinese monk." When they were together, Spielman told Friedlander stories about Asia, and finally Spielman wrote one of the tales down. The result was a total departure from the comedy the men were doing; it was a

In the Kung Fu *pilot, Caine prepares for his first confrontation with a renegade monk sent from China to the Old West.*

story that took place in Asia and that had a character who travels through China and meets a monk from the Shaolin temple. Friedlander loved the story. One day, he was in Manhattan, walking with Spielman on Broadway. They were approaching Times Square when Friedlander had an idea for a movie. He grabbed his friend and said, "Ed, why don't we do an *eastern* western? We can take the monk from the temple and we can place him in the West." Apparently, Spielman's eyes glazed over. Spielman then wrote a complete story treatment of seventy-five pages. From that work, the men produced a 160-page screenplay. Spielman also wrote a 25-page introduction that described *kung-fu* philosophy and the Shaolin temple, as well as the mysticism, training, and spiritual aspects of the martial art.

To succeed as a dramatic vehicle, their story had to present a conflict. "We needed Caine to be a good guy who got himself into trouble because of a particular event," Spielman explains, "and having him kill the emperor's nephew was as good as any. Consequently, Caine became a man who had to deal with life on another level, . . . one which he had not envisioned for himself when he was in the temple."

By the time they were done, early in 1970, Friedlander and Spielman had grand ambitions. Spielman says he was hoping to create "the definitive martial arts theatrical film—to do for the American cinema what the motion picture *The Seven Samurai* [directed by Akira Kurosawa] had done in Japan." Friedlander echoes his collaborator's enthusiasm: "Never in my professional career have I felt the same sense of dedication and mission. During the time we were creating *Kung Fu*, it was our life's work. It was something that had to be done."

Friedlander and Spielman weren't even imagining (not yet, anyway) a *kung-fu* TV series. Spielman explains that a year after they finished the writing, they tried to get an agent. At the suggestion of Fannie Flagg (author of *Fried Green Tomatoes*), Spielman and Friedlander approached the William Morris agency. As part of the process, of course, they needed to submit their work. Friedlander brought along a book of comic material that they had written for performers like Phyllis Diller and Joan Rivers. On a whim, Spielman placed the *Kung Fu* screen story behind the pages of comedy. About a week later, a young agent called and said, "You know that comedy material you sent me? Well, I don't think it's very funny, but that other thing you wrote? *Kung Fu*? Now that's interesting." Not long after, late in 1970, the agent sold the script to Warner Bros. Howard Friedlander and Ed Spielman were suddenly in the movie business.

Warner Bros. acquired the film because, among other things, the studio was interested in using western sets and equipment it already owned but had mothballed because westerns weren't being made much anymore. Despite their initial enthusiasm, in 1971 executives at Warner Bros. decided not to produce the film. Carradine says the problem was that the script was too violent and esoteric for them. The project may also have been too expensive. Warner Bros. might have spent the estimated $18 million on a sure bet, but *Kung Fu* was a risky undertaking.

Later in 1971, Harvey Frand, who served as liaison between the television and motion picture departments at Warner Bros., read the script. He loved the story and the idea. He thought it had great *television* movie and series potential, so he encouraged the television division to look at the material. Frand met with ABC-TV executives to talk about doing the film as one of the network's popular movies-of-the-week. Then, Frand left the meeting and drove back to his office at Warner Bros. By the time he got there, ABC had closed the licensing agreement and was ready to move forward with the film. It was purchased more quickly, says Frand, than any property he had ever pitched. Even so, at that time, ABC still didn't have any solid intention to go into television *series* production.

While all this was going on, producer Jerry Thorpe was looking for a unique made-for-TV movie to produce and direct. He came across the *Kung Fu* script, and with the assistance of writer Herman Miller, he transformed the screenplay into a television film script.

Finally, in December of 1971, filming started. Now, ABC was, more or less, behind the project, despite the rather high price tag for production (approximately one million dollars for the TV version of the movie). At last, the pilot aired. It was a huge success, so ABC commissioned four more episodes—to be aired one per month. After the success of the first three of these four episodes, the network committed to fifteen more episodes, and, as Frand says, "they did so well that I think at that point the network was just ready to run with what what they had. . . . I don't think they completely understood what the show was trying to say. All they knew is that it was a hit and they should keep on doing it."

Once *Kung Fu* changed from a pilot made-for-TV film into a television series, some script changes had to be made. The flashback scenes developed differently than they had in the pilot, and the essential conflict of the series was complicated by Caine's search for his half-brother. The first change was made for philosophical reasons; the second for dramatic ones.

John Furia wrote most of the flashbacks for the series. (When writers submitted scripts for the series, they were asked not to send flashbacks. Instead, the production relied on Furia's talents and a large research department that found relevant material from old Zen stories and other sources.) In the pilot, the flashbacks told primarily of Caine's personal history and how he came to be the man he was. As the series evolved, they became more of a reflection on what he was experiencing or learning in the West. They showed his attitudes toward his current life instead of merely presenting glimpses into his youth. Before a flashback was put in the scene, Furia says, "we resolved it had to have a substantial reason for being. It had to enlighten Caine or be a motivating force or expand on some thought he was having in the present. It also needed to be integrated visually. We didn't want to just cut to a flashback and then cut to the present. There had to be some way that a visual element of the foreground story triggered the introduction of the first shot of the flashback."

Along with the altered flashbacks, the series incorporated a new conflict. As Furia points out, Caine was a reluctant hero. Given the rules of storytelling, this made for a "very difficult protagonist," according to Furia, "because his involvement in the series had to be more carefully and cleverly and creatively designed." This meant, among other things, that Caine needed to have something that he was looking for in America. While it's true, as Ed Spielman notes, that Caine was really looking for himself, it is hard to depict an inner search on screen. Certainly, the flashbacks were supposed to help with that; but the show needed something else. In the first episode of the series, Caine learns from his grandfather that he has a half-brother in America. Once that addition had been made, the essential search, for the rest of the series, was determined. In addition to everything else, Caine is wandering the West in search of his elusive sibling, Danny.

Master Kan (Philip Ahn) invites young Caine (Radames Pera) to "snatch the pebble" in this celebrated scene from the Kung Fu *pilot.*

CHAPTER THREE

The Shaolin Way

I N HIS BOOK *Spirit of Shaolin* (Boston: Charles Tuttle, 1991),
David Carradine defines *kung-fu* as

*an ancient fitness program through which humankind realizes its
full potential through better understanding, learning to set higher
limits and standards, transcending rigid and false values and
achieving harmony with the laws of nature and the universe. Kung
fu is training with a useful purpose, and leads to the learning of re-
fined skills, which will remain with the student for a lifetime, and,
perhaps, even longer.*

Viewers of the *Kung Fu* show were able to absorb some of the
tenets of *kung-fu* by merely following the story. They were also
able to observe some of the practices of the discipline. Among
these is the study and the practice of the Animal styles. The Animal styles form the basis of the *kung-fu* system. In the pilot film,
Master Kan walks through the temple courtyard where men are
demonstrating the various styles. The disciple Caine walks behind
him and observes the ancient movements while Master Kan nar-
rates all that Caine sees, as follows (from the Spielman and
Friedlander original script):

MASTER KAN: In the Shaolin Temple, there are three kinds of men . . .
students, disciples and Masters. The development of the mind can be

Caine's two teachers: the blind Master Po (Keye Luke) and the head of the Shaolin Temple, Master Kan (Philip Ahn)

achieved only when the body has been disciplined. To accomplish this, the Ancients have taught us to imitate God's creatures . . . .
From the Crane we learn grace and self-control.
The Snake teaches us suppleness and rhythmic endurance.
The Eagle, the duality of hard and soft.
The Praying Mantis teaches us speed and patience.
The Way of the Tiger . . . tenacity and power.
. . . And from the Dragon we learn to ride the wind.

The purpose of studying the styles—and there are more systems than the ones Kan mentions—is explained when one understands the basic *kung-fu* tenet that all creatures are one with nature. To study the Animal styles is to perceive nature in an essential way. The idea is to dissolve the mind-body split.

Much of modern Western thought is dependent on the notion that the mind and the body are separate things, but *kung-fu*'s philosophical allegiances are to Taoism and Buddhism, systems of thought that do not distinguish between mind and body. In Taoism, in particular, apparent opposites are not truly opposed but are the same thing, part of the same whole. Thus, mind and body are one, man and nature are one, love and hate are one. All is one. Ideally, mind and body are experienced as one in the discipline of *kung-fu*. Self-defense follows. As David Carradine explains in *The Spirit of Shaolin*, "the confidence and insight which come from gaining the knowledge of one's own body will turn away all but the most determined efforts at aggression with ease." The *kung-fu* student practices the Animal styles, so he or she can reduce conflict and be one with the universe. Clearly, this is no easy task, and Kan, after he describes the Animal styles to Caine, reminds him that "it may take half a lifetime to master one system." And yet, when Caine asks which of the systems he teaches, Kan enigmatically answers, "I teach them all."

Aside from demonstrating the Animal systems, the *Kung Fu* pilot introduced some important *kung-fu* tenets and practices in a few memorable scenes. These include the famous "Snatch the pebble from my hand" scene (described in chapter 1), as well as a scene in which Caine bows to an opponent, one in which he learns to walk on rice paper, and one in which he brands his arms. Even Caine's acceptance of the nickname Grasshopper reveals something about the *kung-fu* system.

Over the years, the cast and crew learned to explain these moments in terms of *kung-fu* philosophy, instead of simply in terms of dramatic meaning.

The nickname Grasshopper, for example, is simply an affectionate term that an older man gives to a younger one. But, Ed Spielman suggests, it is also something more: "Master Po begins to use the term 'Grasshopper' partially as a way to remind young Caine of that first perception [of Po's sensing the grasshopper at young Caine's feet, when Caine could not]." The name reminds young Caine of how far he has to go in learning about life. Simultaneously, it explains how far Po has gone in his own life, despite the fact that he happens to be blind. "Basically," Radames Pera says, "every time Master Po says 'Grasshopper' it's a little trigger in Caine's mind, measuring his place in life."

There's probably even more to it. Praying Mantis is one of the Animal systems. Thus, David Carradine says of the character's nickname, "it's better than locust or cockroach. It should have been 'Praying Mantis,' but 'Grasshopper' sounds better." Pera adds that the grasshopper is a "spring/summer insect . . . in the green blades of grass, always frolicking as the sun shines upon him. He has powerful legs." Pera doesn't think this last fact is necessarily significant. Mostly, he thinks that what is important about the name is that it serves as a reminder for the young man always to be aware of his potential, and this requires being fully awake, fully present to the moment.

Cast and crew also explain the famous pebble scene in terms of *kung-fu* ideology. John Furia argues that "snatching the pebbles was a visual expression of a personal sense of growth." It wasn't merely a matter of reflexive speed. In fact, "from a Zen perspective, when you can accomplish the unaccomplishable, you are ready, you have matured, you are your own person. And so [the pebble snatching] was kind of a metaphor for being grown up."

David Carradine offers a useful analogy for understanding the pebble scene by telling this story of Siddhartha. Siddhartha spends his life looking for the Buddha. Halfway through his life, he actually meets the Buddha in his wanderings and doesn't recognize him. Then he goes through a whole series of life experiences: becomes rich, has mistresses, owns properties. Later he loses all this, and he wanders to a river, where boatmen are gathered on the shore. Buddha is there. He is a ferryman, and Siddhartha finds him dying, and Buddha tells him, "You have to run the ferry from now on." So, even though he didn't know it, Siddhartha had already met the Buddha, and found that he had something of the Buddha within him.

In other words, Caine always has the knowledge he needs, he just doesn't always have the understanding he needs to go with that knowledge. When he can finally take the pebble from his master's hand, then he has what he needs: knowledge, physical agility, and understanding.

Pera particularly remembers the shooting of the pebble scene, because it was done at least fifteen times. He explains: "Every time Philip Ahn [who played Master Kan] offered me the pebble, I was able to take it out of his hand. And I didn't mean to do that. I reached for it sincerely but not too fast. But every time he opened his palm and said, 'When you can take the pebble from my hand, it will be time for you to leave,' you'd hear, 'Cut,' because it wasn't there. And I had this kind of sheepish grin on my face and I'd hold my hand up to the camera and indicate silently, 'Well, here it is in my hand.'" Finally Jerry Thorpe instructed Pera to move his left hand before he reached with his right hand. That way Ahn could see Pera coming and close his hand in time.

Along with the pebble scene, the scene in which young Caine walks on rice paper is one that viewers often remember. Because a Shaolin monk must be humble, he must learn to tread lightly—symbolically and literally—on things. That is, he must learn to walk softly. Some people, says Kam Yuen—who worked on the show and is still David Carradine's *kung-fu* master—practice this skill by stepping on eggs without breaking them. The pilot chose to show Caine practicing this skill by walking on a strip of wet rice paper. Master Kan explains to the young Caine, "When you can walk the rice-paper without disturbing it . . . then your steps will not be heard." The purpose of the exercise, Radames Pera explains, is to learn how "not to raise dust as you move through life." You are practicing, he notes, both grace and stealth, and you are trying to do this with "an attitude of reverence." In the end, the idea behind the practice is that "you leave very little disturbance behind and consequently at the time of your death, your attachments to life are minimized and you may go to the next plane of learning."

Carradine says he also thinks the rice paper is a metaphor reflecting Caine's respect for the earth's surface. Caine could walk barefoot over the ground without causing damage and that meant he was participating, in a way, in the growth of the trees and the grass.

Pera has a funny story about the filming of the rice paper scene. Apparently, when the directors were ready to shoot it, the prop department couldn't find any rice paper. The production people went all over Chinatown and found nothing, so they ended up using butcher's wrapping paper. But the butcher's paper didn't tear when Pera walked on it, and the purpose of the scene was to show that young Caine didn't yet have the skill of treading lightly. The crew glued pieces of sandpaper to the bottom of Pera's feet but that didn't help. Then they instructed Pera to try again with the sandpa-

As Caine (David Carradine) strikes a classic kung-fu pose, he displays the traditional Shaolin branding on his forearm.

per on and to twist his feet as he walked. No luck. In the end, they had to shoot the scene in a completely different way: they tore the paper in advance and had the camera pan down to where the young Caine had just walked.

At the end of the pilot, Caine has to fight the renegade monk, the fellow student at the Shaolin temple who has gone bad. When they fight, they do so in accordance with the "rules" of the temple. They bow, formally, before they begin. Kam Yuen (eventual technical adviser for the show) explains that bowing is a matter of honor and respect. When you bow, you must always look into the eyes of your opponent. If you don't, you are being disrespectful.

David Chow, the show's first technical adviser, adds: "One bows to a master without a gesture of offering, since the master has an abundance of confidence, serenity, and strength. So you just bow with your hands at your side. But if you bow to someone equal or less than yourself—a stranger or an acquaintance—then you may offer them your heart and your strength and you look each other in the eyes." To offer your heart and your strength, you open one hand (to signify your heart) and close the other hand in a fist (to signify your strength). If you don't look into someone's eyes when you are bowing, says David Chow, "you are simply bowing incorrectly. It would be like saluting a general in the American army with just two fingers. That is, quite unacceptable."

Aside from depicting *kung-fu* accurately, the creators of the series took pains to depict authentically the Shaolin monastery in northern China where monks trained, and where the art of *kung-fu* really was developed. The pebbles and the bowing were part of the practices at the actual monastery. The rice paper, according to Ed Spielman, was not a practice that originated at the Shaolin monastery; rather, it was a training device used by *ninja* warriors who needed to learn to move silently. Though *ninja*s were Japanese and Caine was Chinese, Spielman included the rice paper scene because, when it was appropriate, he wanted his script to combine aspects of numerous Asian cultures.

The impressive, and painful, scene in which Caine burns the sign of the tiger and the dragon into his flesh is, David Carradine says, "utterly historical." Shaolin monks really did walk down a long corridor near the temple's exit, and if they were able to get past the dangers of the corridor (for example, the spears sticking out from the walls and the floor, and the acid dropping from the ceiling), they really did brand themselves. In reality, Carradine says, "there was a lot more to a disciple's leaving the temple than just the branding of the arms. We left the rest of it out because we thought nobody would believe it." Indeed, at the real temple, many monks did not make it to the end of the corridor. For those who did make it to the end, there were two options: to lift the urn full of hot coals with the arms or with the stomach. The former required more strength; the latter was probably easier but the pain was greater. David Carradine's kung-fu master's teacher (that is, Kam Yuen's master) was branded on his stomach. "But," Carradine says, "you don't find too many of those people around anymore." The practice, he explains, has been more or less abandoned as barbaric.

*The flute and
flowing hair sported
by Caine (David
Carradine) are in
harmony with his
peaceful nature.*

CHAPTER FOUR

Kwai Chang Caine

L IKE SHANE and other heroes in westerns, Caine was, in part, a mystery man. For the viewer, therefore, part of the potential satisfaction of each episode had to do with the slow revealing of his character. To understand Kwai Chang Caine, it helps to refer, as the writers of the show did, to the description of the original Spielman and Friedlander character, which was penned by Herman Miller. Throughout the run of the series, this description was used by those working on the show:

> *Wyatt, Jesse, Billy—we all know their names. The legends about them are legion. The American West is the cauldron out of which they were born—the western hero.*
>
> *Lawman or Outlaw, they tend to fit a classic form. Loner, moving outside the pale of whatever social order there was, wanderers, driven men.*
>
> *Such a man is Caine.*
>
> *His past is shrouded in mystery; his legend precedes him. Tales are told of his prodigious feats of strength, his endurance, his agility. But such legends bring their own attrition, for there are always men who must challenge the legend, test themselves against it, aggrandize themselves at its expense.*
>
> *As Caine will learn.*
>
> *Rootless, restless, driven by internal and external forces (surely a classic American figure), Caine will never be allowed to*

rest, for close at his heels is a relentless Enemy, whose Imperial
honor can only be satisfied with Caine's death. The wanted post-
ers read: $25,000 dead or alive—to be paid by the Chinese
government.* Bounty hunters, predators, opportunists smelling
the rich treasure awaiting the man who can take him are never
far away. Nor can Caine escape this pursuit, for seared into his
flesh are the signs that must inevitably identify him before the
world; on his left forearm, the sign of the Tiger; on his right, the
sign of the Dragon.

The Marks of Caine.

Caine is a duality. In a way, the familiar western hero, recog-
nizable, satisfying. But in perhaps a larger way, he is unique. He
is a man who seeks peaceful justice in a time of violent solution.
He becomes almost the inadvertent symbol, the unsought-for (on
his part) champion of the underdog, with whom he can empa-
thize only too well—the Red Man, the Brown Man, the Yellow
Man, and the Black. Though he doesn't seek out this kind of action, he yet attracts it, and, being what he is, a man who cannot
endure injustice, he must act on it.

As a traditional western hero, we can see him in traditional stories, but with a new dimension. See him, for instance, as Shane,
drawn to the side of a small family fighting to keep their home
against the incursions of the cattle barons, forming a relationship
with both the man and the woman. The woman, like other women,
will be drawn to him by his air of mystery, his aura of gentleness
combined with strength. And because he is human, and because it
is not forbidden to him, he may be attracted to her.

See him, perhaps putting together a force of Seven Men to
help him defend a small town against the depredations of a gang
of outlaws. On a Stagecoach pinned down by circumstances or
enemy fire, forced to find a way out. He might be the reluctant
Gunfighter, challenged by younger men, facing the Bounty
Hunter, or having to face the unreluctant gunfighter waiting for
him outside any door. Though he is not a fugitive from U.S. law,
any Sheriff or Marshall might find Caine unwelcome, knowing he
will draw trouble; or might find himself needing Caine's special
kind of help.

---

*In the scripts for the series, the reward for Caine was always $10,000 (if he were
brought in alive) and $5,000 (if he were brought in dead). There is no particular expla-
nation for why the figure was changed after Miller wrote this description of Caine.

In the vastness of the West, he may come across a small child, alone. Caine will have to bring him to his destination. A young Chinese woman, won in a poker game, running, stumbles into Caine with her pursuers close behind. A dying man entrusts to him a final legacy to transport. In all of these, he will have a goal and will be in motion.

In Caine is another classic western hero—the tenderfoot; the man out of his element. "What is a railroad?" asks Caine, when it is suggested that he might find work there. "How should I mind it?"

America and the West are new to Caine, Terra Incognita. What is a silver mine? a bank? a cattle drive? a Hanging Judge? What is the hatred between Homesteader and Cattle Baron? between Red Man and White? between the forces of civilization and the vast distances where the only law is made by a gun? How should he mind these? Caine has much to learn about this new country, and learning is frequently a painful experience.

For that matter, it should not be forgotten that Caine is half-American. What legacies, material or spiritual, have been left to him by the American father he barely remembers. Who was his father? What drove him to China? What life did he leave behind in America? Where were his roots? Who were his friends? his enemies?

These are all questions that Caine will have to answer.

With all this we are still left with the richness and the color of Caine's background in the Shaolin Temple. The sets are alive and standing—the inner temple, the temple court. In these settings we will meet Master Po again, following with blind eyes the progress of his favorite pupil. We will see more of Caine's training in Kung Fu, the mystical and spiritual discipline that has made Caine what he is; pursue more of his relationship with the venerable Master Kan, with other pupils, novitiates, masters. We will find Caine strangely modern in his reverence for life; in his seeking to be at one with the forces of the Universe.

For all of these are the mystique of the man who is "known by many names," but whom we all call CAINE.

In analyzing the character, workers on the show tend to concentrate on the meaning of Caine's one great mistake. Ed Spielman explains: "Caine was not a perfect creature, and his killing of the emperor's nephew proved that. It haunted him through the run of the series. And he had to reflect on the justice or injustice of what he had done."

In a certain sense, Caine's error starts with Master Po's admission of his own imperfections. As explained earlier (see chapter 1), in the pilot, Master Po confesses his one ambition—to make a pilgrimage to the Forbidden City, to visit that place on a certain day for a certain festival. This is "bad," insofar as a Shaolin priest should not have ambition. Still, Caine says to his master that this doesn't seem so horrible; after all, it's not such a great ambition. Master Po responds, "But it is ambition, nonetheless. Who among us is without flaw?"

It is at the festival that Po is shot, and Caine throws a spear at the emperor's nephew. In the original script of the motion picture, Spielman says, the emperor's nephew was more obviously evil. In the version that was produced, he's no hero but is not as terrible. This change complicates Caine's personal dilemma, for it's not so clear that he did the right thing. The change also complicates Caine's personality. John Furia explains that Caine was, in his own eyes, a failure, and he was intensely ashamed of killing the nephew. Thus, Furia says, "in a broad overview, you could almost say that his wandering was almost self-imposed because of his failure."

Certainly, others don't view Caine as he views himself. Caine says to the dying Po, "After everything you taught me. I have disgraced myself." Po doesn't agree; he says, "No. Sometimes one must cut off a finger to save a hand."

Viewers probably agreed with Po's interpretation of the killing. Producer/director Alex Beaton says that Caine's act proved "he was human after all. What he did was probably something that anyone would have done in that same situation. And if that sequence is watched closely, it's made obvious that there wasn't any time for Caine to give serious thought to what he was doing. He was reacting to his gut feelings. His action was instantaneous."

Despite Caine's one great mistake, the show was not explicitly about revenge or anger. David Carradine points out that the character never responded to anger in the way that characters in the usual martial arts or action films do. When he was in combat, he never screamed or made any noises, he reacted quietly. He would just breathe. If you look at the fight scenes carefully, Carradine says, you can "observe *gigong* breathing while Caine is punching people." He explains that *gigong*, part of the *kung-fu* discipline, "is a breathing that is done in order to build up your *chi* [inner strength]."

Because the show used different actors to play Caine at different stages in his life, audiences were able to see the character develop. "The young Caine is," Carradine says, "doing what he's told. The adult Caine is deliberately facing the fire in order to confront his destiny." Indeed, the young Caine was unformed and questioning. He was frequently puzzled by what he was told. John Furia explains that the young Caine was used to reflect the audience's possible puzzlement about what was going on in the foreground story. The origin of the puzzle would be explained in a flashback in which one of the masters would say something to the

The young Caine (Radames Pera) in a pensive moment

young Caine. The master's words would resonate with the young Caine and, it was hoped, the audience.

Furia summarizes the three main stages in the character's life by saying that there was "the boy who was a boy, learning, wanting to understand, but frequently puzzled by what he was being taught or what he was experiencing; the teenage Caine who had mastered his lessons but not himself; and then the adult Caine who had mastered both his lessons and himself."

These stages were primarily represented by the actors Radames Pera (the young Caine) and David Carradine (the adult Caine), although David's younger brother, Keith, had a brief stint as Caine in his twenties.

Before filming of the *Kung Fu* TV movie began, there was some discussion as to whether or not an Asian actor should play Kwai Chang Caine. Bruce Lee was considered for the role. (In 1971, Bruce Lee wasn't the cult film hero he later became for his roles in *Fists of Fury* (1969), *Enter the Dragon* (1973), and *Game of Death* (1979). At that point, he was best known as Kato on TV's *Green Hornet* (1966–1967). (*Kung Fu* guest actor Robert Ito reports that Lee hated the role of Kato because he "thought it was so subservient.")

"In my eyes and in the eyes of Jerry Thorpe," says Harvey Frand, "David Carradine was always our first choice to play Caine. But there was some disagreement because the network was interested in a more muscular actor, and the studio was interested in getting Bruce Lee." Frand says Lee wouldn't have really been appropriate for the series—despite the fact that he went on to considerable success in the martial arts film world. The *Kung Fu* show needed a serene person, and Carradine was more appropriate for the role.

Ed Spielman agrees: "I liked David in the part. One of Japan's foremost karate champions used to say that the only qualification that was needed to be trained in the martial arts was that you had to know how to dance. And on top of being an accomplished athlete and actor, David could dance."

Carradine had already played "Third World" and introspective characters on Broadway—starring roles in Rolf Hochhuth's *The*

Deputy (1964–1965) and Peter Shaffer's *The Royal Hunt of the Sun* (1965–1966). On television, he'd played such a part in the short-lived series *Shane* (1966–1967). He had some knowledge of Asian esoteric thought. Nonetheless, Carradine originally declined the project, because he wasn't interested in committing the time necessary for a series. Once he read the script, however, he felt he could hardly refuse.

Still, despite the actor's attraction to the role and the enthusiasm for him in it, there might have been more controversy about casting Carradine, a non-Asian, in the part. Granted, the character was half-Asian, half-Caucasian, so either an Asian or a Caucasian would have been a reasonable choice. (A Eurasian would have been the most natural choice.) Nonetheless, grumbling from the Asian community would have made sense, given the fact that minor roles for Asian actors in Hollywood were already limited, and good major roles for Asian actors were almost nonexistent. James Hong, an actor on the show and ex-president of the Association of Asian/Pacific American Artists (AAPAA), says that at the time, Asian actors felt that "if they were going to have a so-called Asian hero on *Kung Fu*, then why don't they hire an Asian actor to play the lead? But then, as the show went on, we realized that it was a great source of employment for the Asian acting community." In fact, Hong says, Carradine had a good relationship with the Asian community and the AAPAA. One Chinese New Year, Carradine went with *Kung Fu* technical adviser David Chow to dine with the mayor of Chinatown. On the way, he rode, with his then partner Barbara Hershey, and their son, at the front of the New Year's Day parade. Carradine also attended one of the AAPAA's annual awards shows. Feelings, says Hong, were mutually warm.

Apparently, in the end, there really was general agreement that David Carradine was perfect for the role of Caine. Not only did he have, as director John Badham said, "a great lock on the character," but he was able to bring himself to the role in a perfectly believable way. There were some similarities between Carradine and his character. Alex Beaton explains that "David had always been interested in mystery and in the mystical elements of life. And *Kung Fu* was a great opportunity to explore that interest. . . . David was a peaceful guy. He really just wanted to bring joy to

*Kwai Chang
Caine strikes a
kung-fu pose.*

himself and the world. I believe he wanted his life to be as Caine's. In other words, his intentions and Caine's were one and the same. And he had Caine's principles." This similarity was evidenced in many ways. Caine eschewed meat, and Carradine was a vegetarian. Carradine even used to go barefoot, like Caine. Once Carradine appeared on The Merv Griffin Show without shoes. He'd show up the same way—barefoot and, sometimes, in ragged jeans—at formal industry affairs. Carradine says he was not trying to prove a point. He was just trying to be himself.

Through the years, people sometimes conflated Carradine and his character. On the soundstage, workers occasionally said, "I need to talk to Caine," and Carradine would tell them, "I'm not Caine. I'm David Carradine." Fans, also, took David for Caine. There was a period of David's life when he found himself caring—like Caine—for a lot of people who approached him on the street. Finally, he decided he should stop doing that, because he was finding it hard to extricate himself from other people's lives.

When asked to define how much of Carradine is in Caine and vice versa, Carradine says, somewhat enigmatically, "I don't really have an answer for that. I mean, I'm an Irish-American, son of an actor born in Hollywood. And I'm sophisticated certainly. And I'm certainly not a Buddhist monk. I'm also sort of a redneck. I'm a horse person. I collect guns and swords for kicks. And I'm a classical and modern-rock-and-roll musician."

Still, at the height of the series, David had a few problems that resulted from his star status. People would actually throw punches at him. (An indication, perhaps, that not everyone was getting the show's message, that maybe the show was having the opposite effect from the one it intended.) Harvey Frand says that "David was so uniquely charismatic in the role, people were throwing themselves at his car in the street. It reached a point where he wasn't really safe outside the studio and he would have to stay in his dressing room."

All this seems to suggest that Carradine might have been called upon to use the skills that his character possessed (and that he himself was developing). But, Carradine says, he didn't really encounter substantial trouble. "Every once in a while, I would have to demonstrate a technique, but that's it." As to actual combat, he says that when challenged, most of the time he would (like Caine) "see it coming and just walk away." Still, once in a while, he confessed, "I would have to use a technique, but I never had any real trouble to the point where someone really beat me up." As to the wisdom that his character possessed, Carradine says, "I'm not about to present myself as a potential guru." That isn't to say that Carradine doesn't like to help people when he can, for he does. He just tries to be selective about how deeply involved he gets.

For a brief while, as mentioned, David Carradine's brother Keith played Caine in his twenties. After the first segment, however, Keith worried that everyone would think that he had the part only because he was David's brother. (Not long after, he did *Nashville* with Robert Altman and his career took off.) With Keith gone, the majority of the scenes of the young Caine were played by eleven-year-old Radames Pera. Like David, Pera seemed to have an affinity for his role. His mother was interested in theosophy, so Pera had some knowledge of mystical thought, and this gave him a basic understanding of the show's concepts. Still, he says, at the start, his understanding was purely intellectual. He didn't completely "get it" on an emotional and spiritual level; he was too young for that. He was able, however, to turn his youth to the part's advantage and play the character with an appropriate amount of wonder. To fans, it often seemed as though he were really seeking something.

Cast members speak fondly of Pera. John Furia describes him as "a very kind and innocent boy. In that sense, he was very much like the young Caine." Harvey Frand says he feels that the character of Caine had a huge effect on Pera the person: "I think he's grown up to be a very spiritual person, and I believe he was very moved by the whole experience of the show. I mean he really got into that character. He became almost monastic in that part."

Pera had his troubles when he was a young man playing the part, and his experience made him feel that he was like Caine, because he, too, was struggling with something. "I didn't exactly have it easy during that period of my life," Pera recalls. "I was kept from exploring many things that children that age are supposed to explore. I don't mean anything negative; I just feel I was not allowed to develop with the proper amount of social experiences that are usually granted a young boy. For example, I was not allowed to have a bicycle because my mother was afraid that I would fall and hurt my face, which would have put a damper on my career as an actor."

Along with this, Pera was teased by his peers at the public school he attended. His head was shaved bald during most of the series and his classmates latched on to this. Pera reflects: "You would think they would have felt, 'Oh, gee, here's this actor from a very popular TV series, and he goes to our school. He must be one of the most popular kids on campus.' Well, I wasn't. In fact, I was exactly the opposite. I was teased an awful lot. Beat up. Kids would pull books out of my hand. Slap me on the head and call me Eightball." Because he didn't feel he had a friend to take him aside and explain to him that his classmates were just jealous, Pera felt rejected and different. Although painful, this experience allowed him to explore what it meant to be different. In this exploration, he was aided by the very concepts Kung Fu was presenting on TV. Thus, though it caused him problems, Pera says he appreciated the opportunity to play the part, since it exposed him to ideas that other children, and other child actors, didn't know about. "As I was dealing with my personal struggles," Pera says, "young Caine was dealing with his, and both of us were benefiting from Asian philosophy and from what was actually written into the show's scripts."

Caine (David Carradine) shares a smile with the seated Master Po (Keye Luke)—something he might not have been able to do with his other teacher, the formal and formidable Master Kan.

CHAPTER FIVE

Masters and Other Supporting Characters

ASIDE FROM CAINE, the two central figures in the *Kung Fu* TV series were Caine's teachers—Master Po and Master Kan. They had, necessarily, different personalities. Po was a more playful character, and he was a bit of a father figure for Caine. Kan, as the head of the Shaolin temple, was more serious, more distant, and more forbidding. Kan was the symbol of reason. Po was the symbol of emotion. Thus, not surprisingly, there was a certain austerity to Kan and a warmness to Po. Radames Pera explains the difference between the characters: "Kan was actually the Grand Master, or the headmaster, of the temple. So consequently, Kan is more aloof, and he was the master you really approached with the utmost reverence."

Certainly, this is evident in the famous broom scene that takes place in the pilot. In it, Po asks the young Caine to hit him with his broom. At first, Caine hesitates, thinking that it is not right to hit a blind man. Still, Po insists that Caine try to hit him as hard as he can. Caine hits him feebly, and Po orders Caine to hit him harder. Caine tries to hit him with more intensity and Po grabs the broomstick and throws Caine down.

Kan would never have taught Caine a lesson in such a playful manner. Instead, he would walk by, offer his wisdom, and move on. The pilot also has a scene that demonstrates this. Kan asks the impatient Caine how long he has been at the temple. Caine, disappointed by the fact that he has yet to start learning, says that he has been at the temple a very long time. Kan asks him again how long he has been at the temple, and Caine suddenly understands. He tells Kan he has not been at the temple for very long. Caine learns his lesson from Kan, but Kan's manner remains distant. Po—were he to teach the same lesson—would be more casual, more of a friend to his favorite student.

In addition to his playfulness, Po is at great pains to make sure Caine understands why his blindness is not something to be pitied. This may explain a few of the otherwise inexplicable things that happen in the pilot. In the famous scene in which Caine kills the emperor's nephew, an imagined slight against the nephew leads to two deaths. This outcome might seem, at first, excessive. As David Carradine explains it, part of the reason the conflict escalates so quickly is that Po defends himself against the blows of the imperial guards. "With his student right next to him," notes Carradine, "Po acted just like he used to act in the Shaolin temple when he was showing others that even though he was blind, he could still take care of himself."

About the origins of the character "Master Po," writer Ed Spielman says: "My grandfather, Jacob Shapiro, came to America from White Russia. He was a physically powerful man, but in his gentle and sweet way, he had an extraordinary influence on the children in the family. He was a moral and spiritual man. When he died, I was only a teenager, too immature to thank him or tell him how much I loved him. The relationship between Master Po and Young Caine was my way of doing that."

Both the actors who played the masters—Keye Luke (1904–1991) and Philip Ahn (1905–1978)—are deceased. Interestingly, other *Kung Fu* actors—as they remember the men—seem to describe Ahn much as Kan, and Luke much as Po. Says Harvey Frand: "I adored Keye. He was such a wonderful man. I seemed to

WKBW-TV personality Dave Thomas (left) *interviews Philip Ahn about his other self on* Dialing for Dollars *(Buffalo, New York, circa 1974).*

have more contact personally with Keye. I mean, Philip was a very nice man. But I think Keye was much more of an open kind of guy. He was more talkative. On the other hand, Philip was an incredibly elegant man, and most amiable. I just did not have the rapport with him that I had with Keye." Frand's words more or less echo those of other people who worked on the series, though, often, people will add that their memories of Ahn are associated with the Chinese restaurant Moongate, which he owned. Ralph Ahn, Philip's brother, remembers that many children would visit the Moongate. They would approach Philip and ask if they, too, could "snatch the pebble" from his hand. Ralph says that his brother would go out to the back of the restaurant, return with a couple of rocks in his hand, and hold them out for the children. Philip Ahn allowed them to "snatch" the stones, and the children were glee-ful; they left the Moongate thinking they had "done" kung-fu.

Radames Pera thinks part of Ahn's apparent aloofness had to do with his involvement in the totally distinct social scene connected with the restaurant. Still, Pera notes, he got along with both of the actors who played his masters. Of Keye Luke, he says, "he was very well educated, a very warm person, and we had a very fond relationship. His head was filled with incredible stories, and his professional experience and past were just so rich. He was Number One Son in the *Charlie Chan* movies, and he seemed to have tapped into some kind of fountain of youth, because he always looked incredibly young for his age. He used to tell me that his secret was to stay out of the sun. He always carried a parasol with him whenever he worked outside."

Guy Lee, who was the agent for Luke and Ahn and many other of his fellow actors on the show, speaks fondly of both men. Like almost everyone else from the series, he speaks of Luke with intense love: "He really was a great man. I miss him a great deal. He was very compassionate toward other people, very understanding, especially of young people." Lee remembers Luke had a real fondness for the role of Po. Even in real life, he thought of David Carradine as something of a disciple. Luke also took real pleasure in dispensing proverbs from the show to fans who approached him on the street. He loved doing this and loved adding his own personal and humorous commentary to his one-line proverbs.

Both Luke and Ahn were quickly chosen for their roles, but Ahn almost didn't get a chance to play Kan because his leg and hip were badly injured in a car accident just before the shooting started. The producers convinced Ahn that his injuries would not be a problem because his leg would be hidden by the black monk's outfit he would have to wear. Hesitantly, the actor agreed to take the role, and, perhaps, the work helped him to recover. David Carradine reports that people on the series "actually created a whole new way for a *kung-fu* master to sit to accommodate the fact that Ahn had this screwed up hip."

Lee recalls that Philip Ahn had a very strong personality. He was a social organizer, he says—someone who loved to party and who was very personable.

Caine in his signature hat, with frequent guest star Benson Fong

During the series, Luke and Ahn grew to be quite close. They often joked about their respective roles. Says Lee: "Philip and Keye had inside jokes with each other. . . . Sometimes people would talk about certain aspects of the script and Philip would say, 'Don't ask me. I'm not the wise one. You have to talk to Keye. He'll tell you. I just verify everything.'"

While *Kung Fu* did not have a big ensemble cast, there were many actors and actresses who returned, again and again, to the show. Many of these performers—including Keye Luke, Philip Ahn, James Hong, Guy Lee, Soon-Teck Oh, Victor-Sen Yung, Benson Fong, Beulah Quo, Pat Lee, and Mako—knew each other from the East-West Players. East-West was a Los Angeles theater company that was formed in 1965. As the actor Mako explains it: "We used to get together and gripe about the lack of opportunity [for Asian actors] and that turned into an idea about how we

*Caine with
James Hong, who
appeared in eight
episodes of* Kung
Fu *and in the
series' pilot*

should have a place of our own. And that's how the company evolved."

Guy Lee was struck by how many members of the Asian acting community got a chance to work on the series. Alex Beaton, who had a hand in the casting of the series, says that there weren't really that many Asian actors for him to choose from, but each week Lee would send a perfect actor over to the set.

Aside from the regulars, *Kung Fu* had—at the height of its popularity—no trouble attracting topflight talent for guest-starring roles. Many actors either were famous when they appeared on the show or went on to considerable fame. Guest stars on the show included Jodie Foster (at age ten), Harrison Ford, Leslie Nielsen, Don Johnson, Robert Urich, and Victor French, among others.

Frequent guest star James Hong modeling an Eastern and a Western wardrobe

CHAPTER SIX

Behind the Scenes

THE SET. The interior and exterior sets for the Shaolin temple were originally constructed by Warner Bros. for the 1967 film *Camelot*. In 1972, the set was redone for the remake of *Lost Horizon* (1973). It was redressed again for the *Kung Fu* pilot and series. Technically, the Shaolin temple is the castle from *Camelot*, wearing new clothes.

The temple set was located in Burbank, California, and, in the early 1970s, it was the largest indoor set in America. When filming *Kung Fu*, Radames Pera reports, the production crew would fill the entire set up with smoke to create a misty effect for the temple scenes—not always a comfortable experience, Pera remembers, since one day the crew used burning amber, which was extremely unpleasant to breathe. Actor James Hong remembers that the set could also get uncomfortable when the scenes required the use of candles. The candles were to add to the temple's eerie atmosphere. Problem was, they also gave off a lot of heat. Indeed, some scenes in the show were lit only by candles. (Says Harvey Frand: "I really am uncertain about the amount of money they spent for the lighting, but I tell you this: the candle budget must have been tremendous.")

Occasionally, scenes in the temple were simply set on empty soundstages that were dressed up with flowers and candles and artful lighting. Sometimes, when money was particularly tight, the flashback scenes would be lifted out of an old episode, and a new voice-over would be used for the old image.

In addition to filming on the old *Camelot* sets, *Kung Fu* used the Twentieth Century–Fox Malibu ranch, where shows like *M*A*S*H* and *Hart to Hart* were done. This ranch included several western sets, a hanging bridge over a river, country roads, and farms. (The studio has since donated the property to the state of California, which still allows the land to be used for filming—as long as the surrounding wildlife is not disturbed.)

PROPS. One of the famous props of the series was the bag that Caine carried with him. It was the bag that Master Po—on his deathbed—gave Caine. The small prop ended up being an almost bottomless sack. "As the need arose," Alex Beaton explains, "Caine would reach into that bag and come up with any number of props that could help him through a difficult sequence."

The series' other famous prop was a flute that Caine carried. The actual instrument used on the show was made by the actor Michael Greene, a good friend of Carradine's who earned an Emmy Award nomination for his work in the series. "I was living up in Laurel Canyon," Greene recalls, "and I had this wonderful grove of bamboo. I had been making bamboo flutes on and off since the early 1960s. David approached me and said that he needed a good bamboo flute for the series. And then, as I would be making them, he'd give them away—sometimes before he would even use them. So it almost became a joke . . . like some kind of out-of-the-ordinary production line."

Carradine explains that the philosophical reason for carrying the flute was that a Shaolin master is supposed to embrace some sort of art form. Since Carradine is a musician, he thought Caine could play the flute. So, one day, he started carrying the flute around with him during his scenes, and no one argued with him about it. Soon enough, the flute was being incorporated into *Kung Fu* scripts.

FIGHT SCENES. David Chow and, later, Kam Yuen were responsible for working with the stunt doubles to coordinate the *Kung Fu* fight scenes. Given Caine's disinclination to use force, both men needed to be adept at making a fight not look like a fight. Alex Beaton explains that, at the beginning of each fight, the technical adviser had to imagine himself as Caine's character and then ask himself, "What can I do to take the force that's coming at me and redirect it?"

FILM TECHNIQUES AND VISUAL EFFECTS. For a layperson, the two most distinctive film techniques on the show were its use of flashbacks and slow motion (which are discussed in chapter 1). A trained eye might notice some of the other effects that were first incorporated into the series by producer/director Jerry Thorpe. These included filtering and long-lens rack focus. John Furia explains the latter technique: "Jerry used long lenses and lenses that deliberately would not hold the entire scene in focus. . . . So, when the show is viewed, one may notice that there would be sharp focus in the foreground and the background would be totally out of focus, and vice versa." Thorpe also chose to use a rack lens— one that allows camera operators to change focus from one place within the shot to another. That way, says Furia, the director can "deliberately take the audience by the hand, visually, and make them pay attention to what [the lens] is focusing on." It's a tricky technique, says Furia, because you want to be able to use it without making the viewer conscious that you're doing so; you want the viewer to pay attention to the story, not to what is going on with the camera.

Another technique the series incorporated was double and triple printing of an image. That is, one of the film editors took a single image and printed each frame two or three times. The result, says John Furia, had dramatic impact, because it both extended the moment and produced a ragged motion.

Filtering was used to give a scene an atmospheric look. Director John Badham says that the filtering gave "an overall color to the show," a look that was different from the gaudy, MGM-musical look that, at the time, the networks preferred. In the western scenes, there was always a muted look with the various browns of a road, a saloon, and a man's clothes blending into one another.

MAKEUP. The makeup for the series was complicated because so many young actors played ancient men and so many actors with hair played characters with a shaved head. (The shaved head, Kam Yuen explains, is a Shaolin tradition because it "takes away feelings of vanity. When everyone has a shaved head, everyone feels more equal. You care about the way you look but you don't. You eliminate differences and become more humble.")

The late Frank Westmore was the person responsible for the makeup in the series. Although Radames Pera speaks highly of Westmore, Pera says he had no fondness for makeup sessions. Pera also didn't have much fondness for being a bald kid at school, so he was in a quandary. Pera's head had been shaved for the pilot. However, for the first season of the show, he insisted on keeping his hair, so he had to wear a skull cap for the part. This meant hours in makeup and, given child labor laws, not much time left over for actual shooting. In the second season, during his second year at junior high school, Pera was persuaded to shave his head again. But eighth grade was as miserable as sixth grade had been, so he refused to shave his head for a third season.

Now, Pera still describes his sessions with Westmore in grueling detail. "There have probably been some advancements made in the technique and application," he says, "but basically you have to glue spirit gum all along the border of your scalp. That stuff dries very hard, and then there's the latex that's dabbed on over the borderline. So by the end of the day, not only are you all sloshy inside there [from sweat] but when you reach to remove it, there ain't no way that it's not going to hurt. After about two or three days of going through this, your skin gets totally raw. And there isn't any alternative but to stick on the next day's bald cap over the raw skin. . . . Anyone who wears a skull cap, I have a lot of empathy for."

James Hong, who speaks of Frank Westmore with a great deal of affection, has some humorous, albeit uncomfortable, memories about his time with the staff from makeup. One day he came as a visitor to the set, but that status did not seem to matter to the makeup man who rushed over to Hong and started pulling at the skin of his face. As he stretched it side to side, he said, "Oh, thank goodness, I think you have enough elasticity to make you into an old man."

Another central illusion of the series was Po's blindness. To make Po look blind, opaque contact lenses were inserted into actor Keye Luke's eyes. Even off set, Luke would wear them—even though it was hard to see out of them. Tiny holes were drilled in the contacts so Luke could see a bit. Still, they left him nearly blind and without any peripheral vision. Nonetheless, Luke kept them on all day—both because it was too much of a bother to take them out and, apparently, because he felt it helped him get into character.

WARDROBE. For the most part, the wardrobe for the show was fairly authentic; decisions were based on what the wardrobe department could learn about the period from reference books. People often assumed *all* the clothes had "meaning," because they frequently did have some historical basis. For instance, people wondered why the monks in the series wore orange. Some of the people from the series say it was simply because the color looked good next to the bricks of the Shaolin temple set. Kam Yuen says that there was also another reason: "Orange is the color of the sun. Every time the sun comes up, it's another day—a new beginning, a rebirth, en*light*enment."

In the series, Master Kan wore a black robe, and this was presumably to represent his distinction and leadership. The white robes that the disciples wore symbolized literal and metaphorical youth.

Though history books were consulted, personal whims and other considerations also played a big part in wardrobe decisions. Some wardrobe changes were incorporated to serve as benchmarks in the series. (That way, says David Carradine, real fans who were watching reruns could always place the episode in the correct season.) The first major change was the shifting of the color of

Caine (David Carradine) as a majestic master in the original series

Caine's shirt from muddy maroon to saffron. Carradine says this
was done to commemorate the death of Bruce Lee. Later, Caine
lost his signature hat. (It had been a Jimmy Stewart–type fedora, a
hat Carradine says both Thorpe and he wanted Caine to have because Stewart always played a humble character in his movies, and
he rarely wanted to fight anyone. He just wanted to be good, even
when life wore him down.) The loss of the hat was, Carradine says,
to indicate when Kam Yuen took over for David Chow as technical

adviser. Then, when David Carradine began to study *kung-fu* formally, his character started to wear a formal *kung-fu* outfit—a soft black pantsuit and jacket with a black belt, all worn over a white shirt.

Part Two

THE STORIES OF *KUNG FU*

*A man must
walk through life
as Heaven
wills.*

KWAI CHANG CAINE
in the Kung Fu
pilot script

INTRODUCTION

A Guide to the Movie Pilot and the Original Series

T HE *KUNG FU* stories include three decades' worth of made-for-TV movies, television shows, and sequels. Chapters 7, 8, and 9 summarize the sixty-two episodes of the original *Kung Fu* series, first broadcast in the 1970s. Chapters 10 and 11 cover the *Kung Fu* sequels of the eighties and the new *Kung Fu* series of the nineties. Below is a synopsis of the pilot for the original series, as well as a reference guide for the original series' synopses that follow and their accompanying notes, which analyze the individual episodes and provide inside information about the production. The original *Kung Fu's* broadcast history and credit listings, along with the text of the show's "Writers' Guide," are also included in this introductory section. Credit listings for the sequels of the eighties and the new series can be found in chapters 10 and 11.

THE ORIGINAL 90-MINUTE MOVIE PILOT
Title: *Kung Fu*

Original airdate:	**2-22-72**
Original story:	**Ed Spielman**
Screenplay:	**Ed Spielman, Howard Friedlander**

Director:	**Jerry Thorpe**
Producer:	**Jerry Thorpe**
Associate producer:	**Alex Beaton**

Caine's adventure in America begins as he wanders into a western saloon and asks the bartender for "Water, please, if it is not too much trouble." A ruffian named Fuller takes an immediate disliking to Caine and tries to remove him from the saloon. With one blow, Caine sends the lowlife across the room. Fuller pulls a knife and Caine kicks it straight up into the ceiling. Then, he exits, leaving everyone in the bar stunned.

Han Fei, an elderly Chinese man who has observed the incident, takes Caine to a railroad site and gets him a job laying track with fellow Chinese. When Caine helps to unload a wagon, his sleeves fall back to expose the brandings of a Shaolin priest on his forearms. Caine's fellow workers understand the significance of the brands, and they bow to Caine. As they do, Caine reflects back to his first day at the Shaolin temple, when Master Kan gave him the "pebble test."

Back in the Old West, Caine quickly realizes that the railroad working conditions are deplorable and that the Chinese labor gang have, justifiably, focused their anger on their American boss Dillon and his foreman, Raif. Caine notes, too, that the Chinese labor gang correctly sense that the civil engineer for the project—a man named McKay— is their friend. Though the workers do not know it, McKay has discovered a sandstone formation containing gas pockets that may threaten the lives of the Chinese workers—who are using explosives to do their job. McKay presents the discovery to Dillon, along with his suggestion for rerouting the railroad so there will be no danger to the workers. Dillon tells McKay that a detour is economically unfeasible, and he will go ahead and order the workers to blast in the danger area. Furious, McKay leaves the camp with the intent of reporting Dillon. Dillon has Raif follow McKay.

As Caine observes all this, he recalls the day when he was finally able to "snatch the pebble" from his master's hand. Then, Caine's thoughts return to the present, as the Chinese laborers reveal that they have learned that Caine has fled his homeland and that there is a price on his head for murder. Soon after, the laborers also learn that McKay has been found dead. Dillon proclaims his death an accident. While Caine helps dig the grave, he recalls the murder of Master Po and his own killing of the nephew of the Imperial House.

Back in the West, there is an explosion where the men are working—the very explosion that McKay predicted would harm the workers. Thirteen men are killed. The Chinese laborers are ready to fight their white employers. Fong, a vocal member of the group, is unpersuaded by Caine's advice to wait. Fong approaches Dillon and Raif, and Raif calmly pulls a gun and kills Fong. Caine persuades the others not to respond with more killing. "To fight for yourself is right," he tells them. "To die vainly without hope of winning is the action of stupid men. Let one death be enough."

Meanwhile, Dillon learns of Caine's past and, hoping to collect the reward money, ties Caine to the center pole of a tent. Caine escapes. Soon after, Han Fei dies while trying to help Caine. Caine is stricken. Han Fei reminded him so much of Master Po; but there isn't time to grieve, for Dillon has telegraphed the Chinese embassy and a representative of the imperial government is on his way to capture Caine. Eventually, three Chinese men arrive. The smallest of the three is a Shaolin monk who has abandoned the teachings of the temple. Caine and the monk fight and Caine wins. When the fight is over and the laborers are finally safe, one of the railroad workers asks Caine what he intends to do from now on. Caine says he will work, wander, and rest when he can. The railroad worker reminds Caine that he can never rest, for the emperor will continue to send men to America. "They will," the railroad worker says, "search you out." There is a long pause and Caine says, "Then let them find me."

Notes: In the famous scene where Po accidentally jostles the Imperial Nephew on the road and is subsequently murdered, the following conversation takes place between Caine, Master Po, and one of the nephew's guards.

GUARD: (to Po) You dare to touch an escort of the Imperial House?
MASTER PO: Humble apologies . . . I meant no harm.
GUARD: Who are you? Where are you from?
MASTER PO: I am Po . . . lowly priest from Honan Province.

GUARD: (to Caine) And you?

CAINE: Kwai Chang . . . also a priest of Honan Province.

Then, the Imperial Nephew gestures to the guard. The guard slaps Master Po hard across the face. When the guard attempts to slap Master Po's face a second time, Po blocks the guard's wrist and holds it. The guard's hand shakes as Po's finger touches a pressure point on his wrist. Po says quietly, "Even one of the Royal House should not punish an old blind man twice for the same offense."

Additional Credits for the *Kung Fu* **Movie Pilot of 1972**

Caine	**David Carradine**
Dillon	**Barry Sullivan**
Raif	**Albert Salmi**
McKay	**Wayne Maunder**
Han Fei	**Benson Fong**
Hsiang	**James Hong**
Fong	**Robert Ito**
Chuen	**Victor-Sen Yung**
Renegade Monk	**David Chow**
Young Caine	**Radames Pera**
Middle Caine	**Keith Carradine**
Master Kan	**Philip Ahn**
Master Sun	**Richard Loo**
Master Po	**Keye Luke**
Production Manager	**Miles Middough**
Assistant Director	**Richard Lang**
Technical Adviser	**David Chow**
Script Supervisor	**Marie Kenney**
Art Director	**Gene Lourie**
Set Decorator	**Ralph Hurst**
Directors of Photography	**Frank Phillips, Richard Rawlings**
Sound	**Bob Miller**
Editor	**Jack Horger**
Props	**Don D. Smith**
Wardrobe	**Ray Phelps**
Special Effects	**Ralph Webb**
Makeup	**Frank Westmore, Al Greenway**
Hairdresser	**Jean Burt Reilly**
Casting	**Hoyt Bowers**

THE ORIGINAL SERIES

Broadcast History on ABC

October 14, 1972, to November 1972; Saturday; 8:00 PM to 9:00 PM
January 1973 to August 1974; Thursday; 9:00 PM to 10:00 PM
September 1974 to October 1974; Saturday; 9:00 PM to 10:00 PM
November 1974 to January 1975; Friday; 8:00 PM to 9:00 PM
January 1975 to June 28, 1975; Saturday; 8:00 PM to 9:00 PM
    NOTE: All times listed are for the Eastern time zone.

General Credits

Kwai Chang Caine	**David Carradine**
Master Po	**Keye Luke**
Master Kan	**Philip Ahn**
Young Caine	**Radames Pera**
Regular Guest Actors	
(various seasons)	**Richard Loo, Benson Fong, Robert Ito, James Hong, Beulah Quo, Victor-Sen Yung, Soon-Teck Oh**
Pilot and series created by	**Ed Spielman and Howard Friedlander**
First-Season Producer/	
Second- and Third-Season	
Executive Producer/Director	**Jerry Thorpe**
First-Season Associate Producer/	
Second- and Third-Season	
Producer/Director	**Alex Beaton**
Second- and Third-Season	
Producer/Writer	
(first three episodes)	**Herman Miller**
First-Season Story Consultant	
and Writer/Second-Season	
Producer and Story Consultant	**John Furia, Jr.**
Second- and Third-Season	
Executive Story Consultant/Writer	**Ed Waters**
Assistant to the	
Producers/Writer	**Lloyd Richards**
Writers	**John T. Dugan, A. Martin Zweiback, Robert Schlitt, Robert Lewin, William Kelley, Charles Dubin, Stephen and Elinor Karpf, Katharyn and Michael Michaelian, among others**

Directors	**Richard Lang, John Badham, Gordon Hessler, Robert Butler, Harry Harris, Walter Doniger, Marc Daniels, among others**
Technical Advisers	**David Chow and Kam Yuen**
Stunt Liaisons	**Greg Walker, among others**
Set Decorators	**Anthony Mondello, John D. W. Lamphear, among others**
Directors of Photography	**Fred Koenekamp, Chuck Arnold, Richard Rowlings, among others**
Sound	**Richard Roguse, Dean Salmon, Jack May, Ralph Zerbe, Barry Thomas, William Randell, among others**
Wardrobe	**Henry Salley and Western Costumes**
Special Effects	**Joe Unsinn, among others**
Makeup	**Frank Westmore, Thomas Burman, Michael A. Hancock, among others**
Hairdressers	**Virginia Darcey, Mary Keats, among others**
Talent Agents	**The Bessie Lou Agency/Guy Lee and Associates**
Original Music	**Jim Helms**

THE *KUNG FU* "WRITERS' GUIDE"

Each of the original episodes of the series was written in accordance with a manual. The precepts of the "Kung Fu *Writers' Guide*" issued by the Story Department at Warner Bros. Television are reproduced here, verbatim.

I. FORM

a. Scripts consist of four acts, which should be approximately fifteen pages each. There is a two to four page epilogue in every show. Story resolution should always occur in the fourth act. Epilogues must be limited to some comment on the story.

b. We prefer that the dialogue be kept as spare as possible with particular attention being given to character interaction and interesting character activity within the scene.

c. When possible, we prefer at least one "flashback" per act.

d. Caine should reveal his physical skill in Kung Fu at least once in each episode; however, he is pacific not aggressive and should resort to physical action only when there is no other

alternative for him to pursue. He never kills nor maims perma-
nently, but always dispenses with his opponents.

II. CONTENT

    a. Theme: "Good prevails over evil."

We have been elective in our choice of precepts from Confu-
cianism, Taoism and Zen, though Confucian philosophy is
probably the most dominant because it is the most optimistic.

    b. Other than the fact that he is a fugitive and constantly on
the move, there are no obstacles related to Caine's having rela-
tionships with women—the Chinese do not believe in celibacy.

    c. Ideally, stories and scenes should spring from character,
rather than incident. Ambiguities should be apparent in charac-
ter and in drama as they are in people and in life.

    d. We prefer to avoid stories about Indians. It is virtually im-
possible to reproduce the culture of the American Indian with
any sense of reality. Among other things, it was very rare to find
an American Indian who spoke English, while still living in his
own environment. Then, too, the limitations with Indian actors
and extras, as well as authentic accoutrements tend to make ev-
erything seem like musical comedy. However, we have done and
will continue to do stories about a single Indian character seen
apart from his own civilization.

    e. Resolutions should avoid the cloying and the cliché. How-
ever, it is important that they are spiritually uplifting rather than
downbeat or tragic.

Caine (David Carradine) confronts the angry Peter Gideon (Brandon Cruz), a lonely young boy with whom he empathizes in Episode #1, "King of the Mountain."

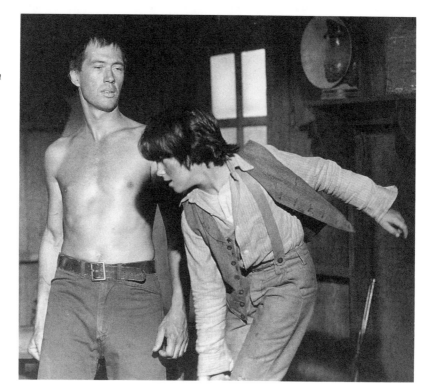

CHAPTER SEVEN

First Season Episodes

Episode number:	1
Episode title:	**King of the Mountain**
Original airdate:	**10-14-72**
Writer:	**Herman Miller**
Director:	**Jerry Thorpe**
Guest stars:	**Brandon Cruz, Lara Parker, John Saxon,**
	Mills Watson, Ken Lynch

OUTSIDE THE smoking ruins of a cabin, Caine finds a dead man and an angry young boy. The boy is Peter Gideon, and he tells Caine that Indians have killed his father and kidnapped his mother. Peter is determined to rescue her. Caine understands Peter's desires, and as he questions the young boy, he thinks back to the day Master Kan questioned him in a similar manner.

MASTER KAN: Where are your parents now?
YOUNG CAINE: Both dead.
MASTER KAN: Have you grandparents? . . . A guardian?
YOUNG CAINE: I am alone, venerable sir.

Peter, however, is not completely alone; he has an aunt in Perrysville. Caine persuades Peter to go there with him. They set off on foot, parting only when they finally reach town.

Peter goes to the post office to find his aunt's address. While there, he sees Caine's picture on a wanted poster. The poster offers a $10,000 reward to whoever can bring Caine in alive. Peter heads to his aunt's house. He finds her slaving over the stove for her husband, Percy McCoy, and their two grown sons, Curry and Frank. The McCoys steal Peter's belongings and then go in search of "the Chinaman." Perhaps he, too, has something they might want.

Meanwhile, Amy Allender, a widowed ranch woman, is outside of town offering Caine a job. Just as she makes her offer, the McCoys show up and Caine, reluctantly, defends himself against the blows of all three. Then, he agrees to work for Amy if Peter may come along. She accepts.

Caine, finding himself attracted to Amy, considers how he should handle his feelings. His thoughts return to the temple.

DISCIPLE CAINE: Master, our bodies are prey to many needs. Hunger, thirst, the need for love. . . . Shall we then seek to satisfy these needs?

MASTER KAN: Only acknowledge them, and satisfaction will follow. To suppress a truth is to give it force beyond endurance.

Caine works at the ranch. His manner is unhurried, but tireless. Clearly, he is at one with nature. He is as comfortable with a wild stallion as he is with Peter, who still needs to learn that it is all right to grieve for the parents he has lost.

While Caine works, he is observed by Raven, a bounty hunter. In a flashback, Caine wonders about fighting. Master Kan advises him to "seek rather not to contend. If there is no contention, there is neither defeat nor victory. The supple willow does not contend against the storm, yet it survives." Still, Raven threatens the safety of the ranch, and Caine is forced to confront him. Though Raven chains Caine's feet with leg irons, Caine fights him and is victorious. It is, however, an incomplete victory for him. He feels his presence will only bring danger to Amy, who has become a surrogate mother to Peter. He explains his departure to her by telling her that people are hunting him. Though Raven is gone, "others will follow."

Notes: In this segment, a few aspects of Caine's character are established. Caine does not eat meat. His essential needs are "food . . . a place to sleep

. . . work." He believes that "a man feels grief. One who does not fails in his capacity to be a man." Caine also displays his sense of humor. "There was," says David Carradine, "always a lot of Stan Laurel–type humor in the character. But many times it was so subtle that it may have gone unnoticed."

Of the guest stars, Brandon Cruz is probably best known as Bill Bixby's son in the TV series *The Courtship of Eddie's Father*. Lara Parker played Angelique, an evil witch in the classic 1960s daytime soap *Dark Shadows*.

Episode number:	**2**
Episode title:	**Dark Angel**
Original airdate:	**11-11-72**
Writer:	**Herman Miller**
Director:	**Jerry Thorpe**
Guest stars:	**John Carradine, Robert Carradine,**
	Dean Jagger, Richard Loo,
	Paul Harper, Adrienne Marden,
	James Griffith

Caine is crossing a desert to get to Lordsville, the place where his father was born. On the way, he finds a dying man, wedged between a split in some rocks. The man is Davey Peartree, a prospector who has been shot. Before he expires, Peartree gives Caine a map to a gold mine.

Arriving in town with Davey's body, burro, and gold, Caine is accused of Peartree's murder. He is saved from lynching by the Reverend Serenity Johnson, a corrupt preacher. Caine gives him the map to the gold mine.

Later, Caine finds Serenity, out by the rocky terrain near the mine. Indians have staked Serenity to the ground, and they have sewn his eyelids back into his brows, leaving his eyes wide open and unprotected from the sun's glare. Serenity is now a blind man.

Flashing back, Caine remembers the words of the blind Master Po: "To be at one with the Universe is to know bird, sun, cloud. How much shall a man lose if he then loses his eyes?" With this wisdom in mind, Caine teaches Serenity to "see" with his other senses. Rescued from despair, Serenity sets out to build a church with money he had been saving for a wild fling. When three townsmen come looking for Serenity, now in possession of Davey Peartree's gold, Caine uses *kung-fu* to protect him and then teaches Serenity how to defend himself in the future.

With Serenity safe, Caine continues his search for his father's father, Henry. Caine finds his grandfather's home, but Henry, embittered by his dead son's marriage to a Chinese woman, will not receive Caine. Caine responds by sitting down in Henry's yard, sitting down by his grandmother's grave. He is prepared to stay there till he dies. Serenity intervenes, accusing Henry of bigotry. "Which one of us," he asks, "is blind?" The two men struggle, but eventually Henry accepts his grandson and tells him that he has a half-brother. Then, he gives Caine some letters from his half-brother. Caine takes them and resumes his wanderings, leaving behind Lordsville and Serenity's new church—the Davey Peartree Church of the Inner Vision.

Notes: The character of Danny, Caine's half-brother, was introduced in this segment to solve a narrative problem. The episode's writer, Herman Miller, explains: "What do you do with a man [like Caine] who doesn't want for anything? How do you handle that in a series? So that's when I suggested the concept of having him look for his half-brother."

Familial ties are clearly significant in this episode. Caine meets one of his relatives, learns the name of his grandmother, and learns that he has a half-brother. Furthermore, in flashbacks, Master Kan emphasizes the importance of roots and filial piety. He says, "The deeper into the earth the roots reach, the stronger the tree." If this is so, Caine is clearly stronger for his visit to Lordsville and, indeed, for his presence in America. Kan also reminds Caine that "much is required . . . in this world . . . respect for country, loyalty for friends, love for family. Of these none is more holy than filial piety, for it is the father who gives the greatest gifts of all."

Given Kan's sentiments, it is perhaps fitting that so many Carradines worked on this segment. David's brother, Robert, played Sonny Jim, Serenity's mute right-hand man. The Reverend Serenity Johnson was played by David Carradine's father, John. (Serenity appeared in two later episodes: "The Nature of Evil" and "Ambush.")

Apparently, John Carradine was never satisfied with his work on the series. "My father," says David Carradine, "did not care for his performance. He looked at it and said, 'I didn't really prove that I was blind.' And that's what he really wanted to do—to act blind. . . . But I thought he was a remarkable performer. I loved it."

The mute Sonny Jim (Robert Carradine, at left) and the blind Serenity Johnson (John Carradine) manage to communicate in Episode #2, "Dark Angel."

Episode number:	3
Episode title:	**Blood Brother**
Original airdate:	**1-18-73**
Writer:	**Herman Miller**
Director:	**Jerry Thorpe**
Guest stars:	**Clu Gulager, John Anderson, Scott Hylands, Kathleen Gackle, Robert Urich, Kermit Murdock, Benson Fong, Frank Michael Liu, Richard Loo, Kam Yuen**

Caine's search for his half-brother takes him into a post office in Kilgore, Arizona Territory. Though there is no information to be had about his brother, Caine notices the name "Lin Wu" on some boxes. Perhaps this is the same Lin Wu with whom he grew up in the Shaolin temple in China? He decides to ask around town. Initially, his quest takes him into a bar where a group of drunk young men are hazing an elderly Chinese man named Soong. They are enjoying his efforts to dislodge the firecrackers they have tied to his pigtail and lighted. They laugh as he slaps at the sparks in his hair. Caine puts a halt to the fun with a single word: "Enough." The young men turn their attention to Caine and begin to move menacingly toward him, when another young man, Greg Dundee, enters the bar and diffuses the tension with some pacifying words to the ruffians.

Dundee advises Caine to leave town—for his own good. Sheriff Rutledge does the same. Caine disregards their advice and stays put. Eventually, Sheriff Rutledge feels compelled to arrest Caine for his own protection. Soong tells Rutledge that no jail cell can keep Caine. Rutledge looks surprised and Soong explains: "A Shaolin priest can walk through walls. It is said that . . . listened for, he cannot be heard . . . looked for, he cannot be seen . . . felt, he cannot be touched."

As Soong predicts, Caine breaks out of jail. Caine then finds Soong's son, Lew, who tells him that the young men from the bar killed Lin Wu and left his body in the marshlands. In a flashback, Caine sorrowfully remembers the combat that his masters in the Shaolin temple arranged between Lin Wu and himself. Presumably, the fight was to see who was the better man. Caine won, but he always felt his gentle friend let him win on purpose.

The men from the bar follow Caine to the marshlands and unwittingly lead him to Lin Wu's body. Rutledge intervenes before they can kill Caine, too. Later, at the inquest, it is apparent the jury is reluctant to bring a murder indictment against the young men from the bar because they feel a Chinese man is hardly human. Finally, however, with the aid of Rutledge, Caine gets the conviction against the young men.

In the course of the trial, Caine tries to understand Lin Wu's death. Lew, Soong's son, asks Caine, "Why did he let it happen? He was a practitioner of *kung fu* like you! Why did he let it happen?" Caine doesn't answer Lew, but he thinks back to his contest with Lin Wu at the Shaolin temple. At that time, Master Kan, in trying to help Caine understand Lin Wu's victory (and subsequent departure from the temple), had said: "Each living thing strives to survive. It is an instinct as deep as life. Yet, Lin Wu, given the ultimate choice of a death, a symbolic death in his contest with you, chose his own. At some time in the future, confronted with the honest choice, he will choose his own. It is, perhaps, the flaw of saintly men, condemning him to an early death."

Notes: This episode directly addresses the racism of the West, particularly the racism against Chinese-Americans. Rather than ignore the complicated rage that results from racism, Caine addresses it head on. Referring to Lin Wu's apparent death, Caine says to Soong: "You are a man. What has happened must make you angry. To hide a feeling is to increase its force a thousand times."

Caine tells people that he seeks "no trouble." At the same time, he asks, "Shall we not look for justice?" Clearly, the search for justice in a racist country will mean that Caine will encounter trouble.

This segment marks the first of several guest appearances by Richard Loo. It also features Robert Urich—now a major star—in a bit role.

Episode number:	**4**
Episode title:	**An Eye for an Eye**
Original airdate:	**1-25-73**
Writer:	**John Furia, Jr.**
Director:	**Jerry Thorpe**
Guest stars:	**L.Q. Jones, Lane Bradbury, Tim McIntire, Harry Townes**

Caine befriends Amos Buchanan and his pregnant daughter, Annie. Together they are looking for Sergeant Straight, who has raped her. Annie clearly has no feeling for the child that is growing inside her, and Caine wonders at her coldness. He remembers the day when he discovered an abandoned infant girl in the courtyard of the Shaolin temple.

YOUNG CAINE: Hunger is everywhere. Is it better to let her die, than force her to live?
MASTER KAN: All life is sacred. Thus the joining together of man and woman is always honored. Apart, there is no life; but from such union, life may proceed.
YOUNG CAINE: Then life must be always defended?
MASTER KAN: The thorn defends the rose. It harms only those who would steal the blossom from the plant.

As Caine, Annie, and Amos travel, Amos falls ill. He has consumption and must turn back. Caine waits with Annie for her brother Samuel to arrive. When he does, Samuel immediately goes to the front to challenge Sergeant Straight to a duel. The two men kill each other, with Annie and Caine watching. This leaves Caine to deliver Annie's son. At first, she will not accept the child and the boy dies, but after Caine has buried him, she is consumed with grief. At the grave, Caine says to Annie, "Before we waken, we cannot know that what we see in a dream does not exist. Before we die, we cannot know that death is not the greatest joy."

Pleadingly, Annie asks Caine, "What can I do?"

Caine responds with one word: "Mourn."

Together, Caine and Annie go back to Amos's cabin. On the way, Caine tries to persuade Annie to forgive the two other soldiers who were with Straight at the time of her rape. "Hate," he tells her, "is the cocoon you weave. It will not protect you from your suffering."

Annie's heart begins to open. Not long after, she is shot by one of the two men she sought to forgive. Caine nurses her back to health, but leaves Amos frustrated and broken by his own hate. "If I don't have the right to revenge," he cries, "who *does*?"

"No one," Caine softly responds.

Rape victim Annie Buchanan (Lane Bradbury) receives some comfort from Caine in Episode #4, "An Eye for an Eye."

Notes: Writer John Furia calls this segment the "No Revenge" episode, and he confesses that it is a favorite of his. He says people often ask about the final line of the episode because "it wasn't the typical response of just any hero. And certainly not the response of a hero in a western drama, or even an American drama." He goes on to explain: "Unfortunately, we believe in revenge in this country, contrary to the Judeo-Christian code. I consider myself a religious man, and I personally think revenge is against this code, as well as against what Taoism and Confucianism are based on."

One of the early questions about the Kung Fu series was whether audiences would like a character who doesn't strike back, who doesn't avenge people who have been wronged. Furia thought that if the shows were done effectively, audiences would love him. "Instead of finding him a wimp," he says, "they would find him a powerfully strong example."

This episode was distinguished with two Emmy Awards—one for the work of cinematographer Jack Woolf and one for Jerry Thorpe's direction.

Episode number:	5
Episode title:	**The Soul Is the Warrior**
Original airdate:	**2-8-73**
Writer:	**Ron Bishop**
Director:	**Richard Lang**
Guest stars:	**Pat Hingle, John Doucette, Shelly Novak**

Still searching for his half-brother, Caine is directed to the Rankin ranch. Caine has been told that the ranchers have some information about Danny's whereabouts. The patriarch of the ranch is out "snaking" (shooting rattlesnakes, that is), but Rankin's son, Breck, is available. When Caine questions him, however, he responds angrily. Later, in town, Caine meets General Thoms and finds out why. Apparently, Danny Caine "took" Breck's girl. Now, the elder Rankin and his son are ready to transfer their anger about this from Danny to the next best thing, Danny's brother.

In town, Thoms ends up shooting Breck in Caine's defense. Breck dies and Rankin comes after Thoms for revenge. Thoms tries to reason things out with Rankin. He does this by going, with Caine, to Rankin's ranch, but Rankin is unwilling to negotiate. His son is dead, after all. When Rankin goes to shoot Thoms, Caine walks over and stands in front of Thoms as a shield. Rankin finds this amusing and amazing. He says to his men, "A cobweb's gonna stop a bullet." And then: "Git that Chinese teacup outa here." Rankin's men grab at Caine, and he throws them all against the walls of the barn. After this, Caine stoically bears a whipping from Rankin, then attempts to bargain with him. He says he wants to trade Rankin's fear for General Thoms's life. Rankin has no idea what Caine means by this. Caine says Rankin is afraid. Rankin says he is afraid of nothing. Caine insists that Rankin is afraid of him. This is a clear challenge. Caine seems to turn away from the challenge, however, because he walks away from Rankin. Soon, however, it becomes clear where he is going—to the rattlesnake pit. Of the snakes, Caine says, "You would not walk among them?" Rankin admits he would not. The scene goes on:

CAINE: And you are afraid.
RANKIN: That'd be the way a fool'd look at it . . . Fool'd put a gun in his ear 'n pull the trigger . . . So what do they put on the headstone? "Here lies a brave man?" Nope . . . just "Here lies another fool."
CAINE: . . . afraid . . .

If Caine will walk in the snakepit, Rankin agrees to let Thoms go free. Caine walks through the pit, and though the snakes curl back as if to attack, none of the snakes strikes him.

Notes: Twice in this episode, a man risks his life for another. First, Thoms protects Caine, and then Caine protects Thoms. These actions require both men to weigh the relative worth of an individual life. The question is complicated by the fact that Thoms *does* kill Breck to save Caine.

In a flashback, Master Kan advises the young Caine: "Seek always Peace. Wear no path for the footsteps of others unless the soul is endangered. We are all linked by our souls. To endanger one, endangers all." But when one is endangered, Kan continues, then the soul must become a warrior. (Master Kan understands the soul to be that which continues after the body's death.)

In this episode, death is a preoccupying concern. Indeed, even the landscape, according to Thoms, seems full of death. When Thoms tries to explain this perception to Caine, Caine says, "Each man sees death in his own mirror."

Episode number:	**6**
Episode title:	**Nine Lives**
Original airdate:	**2-15-73**
Writer:	**Herb Meadow**
Director:	**Allen Reisner**
Guest stars:	**Albert Salmi, Dana Elcar, Royal Dano, Geraldine Brooks, Merlin Olsen, Ross Hagen, Michael Cameron**

Caine wanders into a canyon where several miners are working. These men are prospectors, panning in the river for gold. Caine, working with them, is patiently sawing logs by the side of the river. People are working hard, but they appear to be in a good mood. There is the sound of men singing. By the side of the river, a cat eyeballs a fish. Reaching for the fish, the cat falls into the water and almost drowns, but one of the miners scoops up the animal and tosses it to Caine. He tells him that he's in charge of taking care of the cat. It's a joke, but the man is semiserious, because the cat is the good-luck symbol for the camp.

In considering the activity of the men he is with, Caine thinks back on Master Kan's words: "Wealth by gold alone is a reflection in the eye of another. To know *one's self* . . . that is to be truly wealthy *without* gold."

Back at the camp, Shawn Mulhare, a prospector, dynamites a rock outcropping and finds what he thinks is gold. The cat is killed in the blast, and after a mock trial, Shawn and Caine are sent to town to replace the cat.

On the way, they are robbed by Henry Skowrin and his three sons, including his very large son Perlee. Nonetheless, Shawn is able to hide a "nugget" that he took from the camp.

Later, Caine and Shawn reach the outskirts of town and come across the small ranch of Widda Tackaberry. She has a cat that fits their needs. However, she is unwilling to part with it unless the men dig her a well—for the hotel she dreams of opening.

Meanwhile, in town, the Skowrins see a "Wanted" poster for Caine. Hoping to win the $10,000 reward, they come looking for him and find him digging with Shawn. Caine fights and defeats Perlee, and the widow sends the rest of the Skowrins packing. In the process of the fighting, it is revealed that the "nugget" that Shawn has is really iron pyrite—fool's gold. Shawn, disappointed, decides to turn on Caine. If he can't have a gold mine, at least he can have a $10,000 reward. Caine is at the bottom of the well hole, and Shawn, while considering what he will do, is at the top. Then Shawn falls in and while both men are climbing out, the timber at the wellhead breaks. The rope to climb out falls down and water starts to fill the hole. Back to back, Shawn and Caine inch up the hole. Caine grasps a new timber placed at the top of the hole by the widow and saves himself and Shawn. Shawn repents of his greedy thought, and Caine continues on his way, leaving Shawn and the widow to dream of building a hotel together.

Notes: This episode opens with Caine soothing a cat who has almost drowned. Later, we again get to see Caine's fondness for animals, as well as his skill in taking care of them. Caine helps a pregnant mare and thinks back to an early lesson from Master Po. At the temple, by a candle-lit table, Po and Caine are caring for a wounded dog. Po tells Caine that it is time for him to start to study the nerves of beasts. The scene continues:

YOUNG CAINE: I am grateful, Master Po. I am anxious to know how to control pain.
MASTER PO: You will also learn how to bring pleasure, because pain and pleasure are like two bells, side by side, and the voice of each makes a trembling in the other. There are nerves which can bring on an illness of the body, or of the spirit, and those which can restore health. These nerves are like millions of tiny rivers, and to master these rivers is to be master of the body through which they run.

Episode number:	7
Episode title:	**The Tide**
Original airdate:	**2-1-73 (Aired out of sequence)**
Writer:	**A. Martin Zweiback**
Director:	**Walter Doniger**
Guest stars:	**Andrew Duggan, Mako, Robert Donner, Tina Chen**

A rancher named Houlton recognizes Caine as a man wanted in China. Houlton enables Sheriff Boggs to capture Caine, but then Boggs kills Houlton, so he won't have to share the reward. Boggs tries to kill Caine, too, but Caine foils the sheriff with *kung-fu*. Caine escapes, but he is wounded. Soon after, Caine encounters Su Yen. She also recognizes him, and she takes him home to tend his injury. Caine talks with her and learns that her father, a noted writer, is imprisoned in China. Su Yen seems good-hearted but her motives are dark. Leaving Caine in her home, she secretly telegrams her brother, Wong Ti, who lives in China.

On her return from the telegraph office, Su Yen takes Caine to a hideout cave by the sea. Although Caine doesn't fully trust Su Yen, his illness leaves him no choice but to go with her. Through the night, he struggles with a high fever and she tends to his wound. By the morning, it is clear that they are attracted to one another and that Caine, though still suffering a bit from his wound, feels exuberant because of this attraction.

While Caine remains hidden in the cave, Su Yen goes to meet her brother and his henchmen at the train. Meanwhile, Sheriff Boggs, suspecting her of harboring Caine, follows her, her brother, and the henchmen to the cave. The men from China try to capture Caine but he overcomes them with *kung-fu*. Su Yen points a gun at Caine and says she will deliver him to the emperor in exchange for her father. After she says this, Wong Ti takes the gun from her, and she goes to shield Caine with her body. Just then, Boggs shoots from where he is hiding. The Chinese henchmen flee and Wong Ti falls. Before he dies, he tells his sister that their father is dead, and his own interest in Caine was motivated by greed. He, too, wanted the $10,000 reward.

Boggs appears and aims his gun at Caine, but Su Yen kills the sheriff with a *tong* ax left by one of the henchmen. As they part, Su

Yen sorrowfully quotes her father: "Love born of betrayal is better lost than lived."

Notes: In a flashback, young Caine is taught to reconcile an understanding of the evil in this world with the dictum that one should trust one's fellow man.

MASTER KAN: Deal with evil through strength—but affirm the good in man through trust. In this way we are *prepared* for *evil*, but we encourage *Good*.
YOUNG CAINE: And is Good our great reward for trusting?
MASTER KAN: In striving for an ideal, we do not seek rewards; yet trust does sometimes bring with it a great reward—even greater than Good.
YOUNG CAINE: What is greater than Good?
MASTER KAN: Love.

Episode number:	**8**
Episode title:	**Sun and Cloud Shadow**
Original airdate:	**2-22-73**
Writer:	**Halsted Wells**
Director:	**Robert Butler**
Guest stars:	**Morgan Woodward, Aimee Eccles, Soon-Teck Oh, Ronald Feinberg, Richard Lawrence Hatch, Dennis Lee Smith, Bill Ryusaki**

A Chinese man named Ying is killed in a saloon brawl by Doug Binns, son of the rancher Colonel Binns. Led by a Chinese girl, Cloud Shadow, Caine takes Ying's body to a nearby village of Chinese miners. Recently, the miners have found gold on their land, but Colonel Binns has claimed the land as his own, so the Chinese have twenty-four hours to evacuate. Complicating the resentments that have formed over the killing in the saloon and the eviction is the fact that Cloud Shadow is in love with Dave Binns. Dave is Doug's brother and Colonel Binns's younger son. The two would like to marry, but the colonel will not let them.

As the land dispute seems likely to continue, Caine intervenes. "I am a man of peace," he explains to Colonel Binns. "They have asked me to offer a settlement." Caine is able to persuade Binns to accept the Chinese offer of gold royalties for land. Colonel Binns finally agrees, but then Ying's son kills Doug, and Binns tears up the agreement.

Colonel Binns confronts the Chinese at a barricade and says he will accept their agreement only if they give up Cloud Shadow to be his son Dave's mistress. Earlier, she had told Caine that she would not do this. She loves Dave, wants to be his wife, but not his mistress. Before, when union without marriage seemed the only option, she had left Dave. Now, Cloud Shadow regretfully agrees to be Dave's mistress. To her it seems the only way to prevent death on both sides. But Caine has other ideas.

CAINE: No man can see through another's eyes or hear through his ears, or feel through his fingers. Yet I know your anguish. Your heart is kind. Your love pulls you . . . but with that same love and that same kindness . . . you had the courage to leave, rather than debase yourself.
CLOUD SHADOW: I respect what you say . . . and yet . . .
CAINE: Respect first, yourself.

Caine goes on to say—and clearly he says it for Dave's benefit— that a man faced with two courses must choose one. Dave makes his decision and accepts disinheritance to marry Cloud Shadow and live with her in her village.

Notes: A significant side plot of this episode involves a Manchu karate master who comes looking for Caine. This offers viewers a chance to see how karate differs from *kung-fu*. Karate is a Japanese system derived from *kung-fu*. As David Carradine writes in his book *The Spirit of Shaolin*, the Japanese system is "flashy, monolinear, specifically limited to no-nonsense techniques yielding immediate results." Some of this is immediately apparent in the fight between Caine and the Manchu. Caine's movements are beautiful and flowing. The Manchu's movements are more staccato. He darts at his opponent and gives out sharp cries and an occasional hideous howl.

Episode number:	9
Episode title:	**A Praying Mantis Kills**
Original airdate:	**3-15-73**
Writer:	**Richard Lewin**

Director: **Charles Dubin**
Guest stars: **Wendell Burton, Don Knight,**
                       Norm Alden, Jason Wingreen,
                       Murray Macleod, Bill Fletcher,
                       William Schallert, Victor-Sen Yung

Hap Darrow and his gang rob the local bank, kill Mrs. Roper and
threaten to kill anyone who reveals their identities. Caine, honest
and fearless, is witness to the crime. The sheriff comes to question
the witnesses and Caine's mind fades back to the garden of the
Shaolin temple, to a conversation he had with Master Po.

MASTER PO: The monarch butterfly rests itself on the young cherry
blossom.
YOUNG CAINE: You are blind. How do you see this, Master?
MASTER PO: I see it with my history. I smell it is spring. I know the
monarch loves the cherry. I feel the flutter of disturbed air. All this
speaks to me.
YOUNG CAINE: Sometimes I feel strange . . . You make it seem
better to be blind.
MASTER PO: You are learning.

Back with the sheriff, Caine offers his description of the
criminals. The sheriff's handyman, Victor, tells the bandits
about Caine's disclosure. Furthermore, Victor tells the bandits
that Caine is working at the sheriff's ranch. The bandits lay
siege to the ranch. Caine refuses to take a gun to defend himself.
This surprises Martin, the fifteen-year-old son of the sheriff. Indeed, Martin, though drawn to Caine, thinks Caine is a coward
for this refusal. In the ensuing fight, one of the bandits—named
Darrow—is captured. The price for the capture is high: the sheriff is killed.

Martin and the widowed Mr. Roper try to guard Darrow in
his cell, but the other bandits set the jail on fire. Roper is
wounded. Martin throws his keys into the flames of Darrow's
cell. Caine comes out of the darkness and disables the attackers.
Martin is venting his pent-up hate on Victor, who has tormented
Martin for years and who has also killed his father. Caine calls
Martin off and Martin confesses, "I wanted to beat that Victor to
a pulp . . . But I didn't."

Caine nods and smiles, then says, fondly, "Because, Martin, there is something good in you."

Notes: In this episode, Caine says, "I belong to myself," but later confesses, "I have been lonesome." The lonesomeness is a point of connection between Caine and Martin. The boy feels unhappily alone in life. This echoes a scene from the *Kung Fu* pilot, a scene that is edited into the third act of this episode. In the scene, the boy Caine is standing outside the huge doors of the Shaolin temple. He is bareheaded and waiting, in the rain, for admission and an interview. The other boys with him cluster under the eaves and try to find shelter from the rain. Then, a disciple brings Caine to Kan.

MASTER KAN: You stand in the rain. You do not play games.
YOUNG CAINE: My parents are dead. I am alone.
MASTER KAN: Is that why you want to join us?

Caine shakes his head yes, for this is the case. Then, Master Kan reminds him that even in groups, we are all alone. He says, "Man, like the animals, is meant to live in groups. But the meaning of belonging to a group is found in the comfort of silence and solitude."

Episode number:	**10**
Episode title:	**Alethea**
Original airdate:	**3-22-73**
Writer:	**William Kelley**
Director:	**John Badham**
Guest stars:	**Jodie Foster, Khigh Dheigh,**
	Ken Tobey, Charles Tyner,
	Byron Mabe, Bill Mims

Caine meets Alethea Ingram, an intelligent twelve-year-old girl who is waiting for a stagecoach to go by. While she waits, she plays a rather difficult piece of music on the mandolin. It is the sound of her music that draws Caine toward her, but as they talk it is clear they have something else in common: a certain innocence.

When the stagecoach shows up, there is a holdup. During the robbery, the stage driver throws a gun to Caine. Caine quickly discards the weapon, but before he does, the stagecoach's guard is shot dead by the robbers. The action is quick, and Alethea's perspective is jarred. She believes Caine is responsible for the killing. Caine wants to protect Alethea by not challenging her sense of the truth, so he does not try to persuade her otherwise.

In jail, Caine finds another friend in Alethea's father, who also happens to be the sheriff. The sheriff suggests Caine retain an attorney. Caine replies with good counsel of his own: "If the jury will not see innocence in my eyes . . . will they find it in a lawyer's mouth?"

During all this, Caine remembers Master Po's words: "Guard, above all things, the purity of your vision." The words seem appropriate enough as Caine's case comes to court. Alethea offers what she believes to be true testimony. As a result, Caine is convicted and sentenced to be hung from the gallows in the square. As the hanging is about to take place, Alethea screams from her window, "Nooo!" She runs into the street and cries, "I lied! I didn't see him shoot! I was lying! I didn't see anything . . . I lied . . . I lied . . . 'cause he's a Chinaman . . . I didn't see *anything*!"

Alethea remains confused, though she seems to know, in her heart, the truth. In the end, Caine tells her, "The truth is you are not a liar, and I am not a murderer." Then he tells her that "the people of the country of Greece have a name for truth." She asks what it is, and he says, "Alethea . . . Alethea is a girl who loves truth." Then, the episode ends with these lines:

ALETHEA: I love you, Mr. Caine.
CAINE: And I, Alethea, have never loved anyone more . . .

Notes: A number of people who worked on the show have distinct memories of this episode or cite it as their favorite of the series. There are many reasons for this: people like the message of the episode; they were, to a person, impressed with the intelligence and talent of the young Jodie Foster; and they like this show's visuals.

Of Jodie Foster, who played the title role, David Carradine says, "All we knew is that there was this little girl on the set who was incredibly talented beyond her years. We didn't realize that we were dealing with someone who would become an icon in the industry."

Radames Pera remembers being struck both by Foster and by this particular show. Of Foster, he says: "She was the only other young person who ever guest-starred on the show for a period of consecutive days. . . . So we got to hang out together . . . and we still bump into each other every once and a while."

Director John Badham remembers this episode partially because of rain. "It never rains in Southern California," he explains, "or it rains so seldom, that it's always an occasion for great comment. And people don't like to work in the rain here. Construction workers shut down, movie companies go into a panic. I grew up in England. Very well aware of how to shoot in intemperate climates. So I show up in the morning with an assistant director—his face this mask of grief at seven in the morning because it's pouring rain. He said, 'What are we going to do?' And I said, 'Look, we're shooting a hanging in the rain. Get me some umbrellas. . . .' And I thought this could not have been a more wonderful thing to happen. . . . To be able to have had David walking through this gray, gloomy atmosphere walking up the steps to the gallows, and having his point of view as the noose goes around his neck. And we even put the noose around the lens of the camera. Every hokey trick I could think of to make the audience feel like we're a part of this . . . we're going to get hanged, too."

Episode number:	**11**
Episode title:	**Chains**
Original airdate:	**3-29-73**
Story:	**Paul Edwards, Gene L. Coon**
Teleplay:	**Gene L. Coon**
Director:	**Robert Butler**
Guest stars:	**Michael Greene, Warren Vanders,**
	Geoffrey Lewis, Larry Bishop,
	Keith Carradine

Still searching for his half-brother, Caine is arrested at an army post and chained to Danny Caine's mining partner, a hulking man named Huntoon. Huntoon is charged with killing another man, but he claims he's innocent, that a man named Meader is the one who did the killing. Then, he says that if Caine helps him escape, he will take him to Danny. So, literally linked, the two men break out of jail and flee into the mountains, with Sergeant Bedford hot on their trail.

As he tries to understand Huntoon, Caine remembers Master Kan's words: "Ten million living things have as many different worlds."

Caine and Huntoon first reach a cabin owned by the latter's brother-in-law, Johnson, a man Huntoon hates. Huntoon tries to kill Johnson, because Johnson used to beat his wife, Huntoon's sister. Caine stops Huntoon, and then he forces Johnson to cut the chains that bind him to Huntoon. Huntoon and Caine proceed on their way. Huntoon now confesses that he has killed several times; he has killed when people laughed at him. Indeed, he says, most men do laugh at him because he is "dumb." Caine, however, sees another side of Huntoon, especially when he observes Huntoon's gentleness with a trapped deer. He tries to help Huntoon see in himself what Caine sees in him.

HUNTOON: Can't read or write or nothin'.
CAINE: You know pain and fear . . . You know the laughter of wind and the perfume of the earth . . . Many things you know.

Caine and Huntoon continue on their way till they reach the mining cabin where Danny was staying. Here, they find some gold and traces of Danny, who is nowhere in sight. Then, Sergeant Bedford shows up. Caine overpowers him, but when Bedford tells Huntoon that Caine is wanted for murder, and that he will give him gold and freedom in exchange for help, Huntoon turns on Caine. Then, Bedford reneges on his deal, and Caine and Huntoon tackle him. Huntoon is wounded in the fight, and Caine straps the unconscious Huntoon to Bedford's horse and goes looking for help. Meanwhile, Indians surround the cabin and kill Bedford.

Later, after Huntoon has grown stronger, he decides to remain "unchained" in the wilderness, surrounded by the creatures whom he loves and far away from the people with whom he cannot cope.

Notes: Michael Greene, the actor who played Huntoon, says that making this episode "was an amazing experience. We filmed it on the [Twentieth Century–Fox Malibu] ranch out in the countryside. And usually, after everyone else on the set had gone home, David and I just ended up sleeping outside. I mean, it was quiet and soothing, and we both lived in Laurel Canyon [quite a distance from the shooting location]. So instead of carpooling, we just stayed put."

Of the episode's story, Greene says, "Like a lot of the episodes of Kung Fu, this one had a good message." That message begins when Caine tells Huntoon not to waste his "strength in struggling," and is underlined by Master Kan's words: "See the Way of life as a stream. A man floats, and his way is smooth. The same man, turning to fight upstream, exhausts himself . . . . To be One with the Universe, each must find his true path . . . and follow it."

Episode number:	**12**
Episode title:	**Superstition**
Original airdate:	**4-5-73**
Story:	**David Moessinger**
Teleplay:	**Ed Waters**
Director:	**Charles Dubin**
Guest stars:	**Roy Jenson, Ford Rainey,**
	Fred Sadoff, Don Dubbins,
	Woodrow Parfrey

Convicted of a theft he didn't commit, Caine is put to hard labor in a silver mine burrowing into an Indian graveyard. In the past, the graveyard has always been protected by the legend that he who disturbs the bones will die before sunset. Discounting the legend, Caine works diligently, saying, "I will rest only if I cannot go on. Until then, I will work."

The prisoners' leader, Rupp, notices that the other prisoners are drawn to the strange new man in their midst. Jealous, Rupp attacks Caine, and Caine quickly turns him away with the art of *kung-fu*. Then, Caine and another prisoner are imprisoned in an outdoor pit whose intense heat and cold have destroyed previous occupants. Caine helps the other man survive by teaching him what he has learned.

CAINE: I tell you that you are not within this prison . . . it is within you. Do you believe that?
GIL: I believe it.
CAINE: Then you will direct yourself so that the instrument of your body can no longer be played upon by heat or cold . . . or thirst. . . . Let all effort flow out of you. The weight of your body will become less . . . and less and less . . . until the body is one with the spirit—

which has not even the weight of a feather . . . nor that of a breath . . . of a moment . . . of a thought . . . of nothing at all.

The two prisoners emerge from the pit and are as healthy as ever. Thus, Rupp's leadership passes to Caine, and Rupp's jealousy seems to be transferred to the mine operators, Sterne and Bannack.

Not long after, a miner's pick uncovers bones and a falling beam immediately kills the miner. The prisoners rebel but Caine goes back to work. Observing Caine, the prisoners follow him. This should please the avaricious mine operators, but instead they are nervous. Clearly, this strange Chinese-American fellow has a lot of power over the prisoners. Therefore, they arrange for an accident, which traps the workers in the mine. The men panic, thinking that they have been cursed by their presence near the graveyard, but Caine calms them, teaching them how to conserve air till the entire group is rescued.

Master Po's words have been borne out by the events of the episode: "Superstition is like a magnet. It pulls you in the direction of your belief."

Notes: Some signature lines that appear repeatedly in the *Kung Fu* series are spoken in this episode. There is Caine's laconic introduction, "I am Caine." His reminder that he eats no flesh. Also, there is his questioning of a word he doesn't understand. "What is cooperate?" he says here. Elsewhere, he has asked the same question, but changed the word (for example, "What is ranch work?"; "What is snaking?") The questions show the natural superficiality of Caine's knowledge of American ways and language. He is, after all, an immigrant. The gaps in his knowledge suggest weakness, ignorance; but ironically, even without this information—or the necessary bit of vocabulary—Caine understands more than anybody and is the strong man.

Episode number:	**13**
Episode title:	**The Stone**
Original airdate:	**4-12-73**
Writer:	**A. Martin Zweiback**
Director:	**Robert Butler**

Guest stars: **Moses Gunn, Gregory Sierra, Kelly Jean Peters, Kiel Martin, Ike Eisenmann, Bill Lucking**

Issac Montola, an expert in the Brazilian self-defense technique of *capoeira*, scuffles with some local delinquents. He handles the three bullies well, till one of them, named Quade, draws a gun; then Caine intervenes to offer his help.

During the fight, Issac drops a pouch containing a stolen diamond. He goes to the sheriff to tell him about his loss. The two men argue and Issac knocks the sheriff down, accidentally killing him. Then, Issac goes looking for Caine, who he suspects might have the gem.

It turns out that the gem was pocketed by a small boy named Harpy Lovitt. Harpy is one of three brothers far from home who offer Caine $4.80 to kill Zolly, the saloon piano player. The reason the boys make the request is that they know their mother is planning to kill Zolly, for breach of promise. They don't want their mother to go to jail, so they figure they'll get someone else to murder him.

It turns out that the problem is that Zolly cannot marry the children's mother, because he feels that he must fight for his oppressed people in Armenia. Caine says: "I understand injustice and cruelty. But if you fight them anywhere, do you not fight them everywhere?"

"For me there is only Armenia," Zolly answers. "Someday I will return." Still, he agrees to help Caine return the boys to their mother, Martha, who lives ten miles outside of town. When Zolly sees her, he falls in love all over again, and asks her to marry him.

Then, Issac shows up. Caine and Issac fight. In the midst of their confrontation, Quade appears. One by one, Caine, Zolly, Martha, and her boys step in the line of fire to save Issac, who is eventually arrested by the marshal.

Notes: As in other episodes, Caine makes comments or asks questions that lead to a definition of "man." Here, he says to Issac, "Surely a man like you does not feel less a man for having lost a piece of stone?"

Also, we see Caine's playfulness. When one of the young boys asks him if he likes piano players, Caine says, "I have heard some who pleased my ears and others who did not." As he responds to the boy, his fondness for children is evident. Clearly, children are kindred spirits for Caine.

Episode number:	**14**
Episode title:	**The Third Man**
Original airdate:	**4-26-73**
Writer:	**Robert Lewin**
Director:	**Charles Dubin**
Guest stars:	**Ed Nelson, Fred Beir,**
	Barbara Stuart, Sheree North

Caine becomes entangled in a romantic triangle. The points of the triangle are Jim Gallagher, his wife Noreen, and Sheriff Raha.

Entrusted with Jim's billfold, Caine is held up in a barn. Earlier, he had hidden Jim's money under a rain barrel outside the barn. Inside, as he is confronted by several men, he remembers a time when he was standing in the courtyard of the Shaolin monastery. As an exercise, two students from the temple were advancing on him, and Caine was learning to fight from Master Kan. Kan said: "Training in the martial arts is for spiritual reinforcement. But it is based on self-defense. Disciple Caine, when you are attacked by more than one person, the enemy should be allowed to make the first move and thus create the beginning of his downfall."

As Caine thinks of these words, Jim comes to his rescue, only to be shot by a man cloaked in darkness. Later, Caine realizes this man must be Sheriff Raha. (Caine sees Raha's silhouette as he steps into the barn, and later, he recognizes Raha's profile.)

Caine returns the billfold to Noreen. The sheriff, wanting to appear innocent in Noreen's eyes, demands that Caine tell him what else he knows—aside from where Jim's money was. "I want the truth," the sheriff demands. Caine tells him that he will discover the truth, but not from him. Finally, the sheriff confesses to the crime, but says he did it in self-defense. Then, he goes off to resign his post. While he is gone, Noreen asks Caine to tell her what he saw, to tell her the truth.

Caine confers with a wise Indian elder (Chief Dan George) on the importance of one's heritage, in Episode #15, "The Ancient Warrior."

Caine answers: "I saw a man shoot a gun, but I could not see into his heart." Thus, he leaves Noreen wrestling with the problem of whether she should trust the man she loves.

Notes: In this episode, Caine—who has seen such violence— says, "I do not know why anyone would want to kill anyone." He also talks sympathetically to Noreen about her contradictory emotions for her gambling husband. Caine seems to understand both her love and her anger and, perhaps because of his grasp of Taoist principles, how the two emotions are often one and the same.

Episode number: **15**
Episode title: **The Ancient Warrior**

Original airdate:	**5-3-73**
Writer:	**A. Martin Zweiback**
Director:	**Robert Butler**
Guest stars:	**Chief Dan George, Denver Pyle,**
	Victor French, G. D. Spradlin,
	Will Geer, Gary Busey

Caine travels to a sacred burial ground with Ancient Warrior, a dying Indian, the last of his tribe. Unfortunately, a town has sprung up on the burial ground, and the residents are particularly hostile to Indians. They trace their anger to losses suffered during Indian battles long ago.

Hoping to reach a compromise with the town's residents, Caine convinces Ancient Warrior to attend a town meeting. Speaking in ways even Caine's masters would approve of, Ancient Warrior asks an embittered attendant, "Why can you not try to forget—and discover the sweet solace of forgiveness as I have?"

With Judge Marcus recalling the loss of Indian lives to the townspeople (who seem only to be aware of white history), Ancient Warrior is granted his burial spot.

"It is a hollow victory," Ancient Warrior tells Caine. "This place is filled with hatred." Then he asks Caine to take him away from town. "I want," Ancient Warrior explains, "to die in a pine-filled forest—near the things I have grown to love."

When the old man dies, Caine cremates the body and spreads Ancient Warrior's ashes through town. It is his hope that the act will be seen as a way of purging hatred with forgiveness.

Notes: David Carradine believes that of all the world's religions, Confucianism and "the [Native] American idea of the Great Spirit and 'being one with the Universe'" are the closest concepts to the Shaolin philosophy employed on *Kung Fu*. Episode #15 bears this out, particularly when it shows the strong feelings that Ancient Warrior and Caine have for each other.

This episode was full of actors well-known—or soon to be so—for their other work. Chief Dan George, in the title role, gained fame with film roles in *Little Big Man* and *The Outlaw Josie Wales*. Gary Busey also went on to become a movie star in *The Buddy Holly Story*. Others in the cast found success on television, including Victor French (*Highway to Heaven*) and Will Geer (*The Waltons*).

Chief Dan George wore glasses all through this segment. Carradine says that he had to have them because he wouldn't learn his lines; he needed the glasses so he could read the cue cards. Says Carradine: "I guess at his age, he had a right to be arrogant . . . after he had played so many great parts. Shit, Marlon Brando won't learn his lines. Jack Nicholson won't learn his lines. So why should Chief Dan George?"

Caine (David Carradine) fighting after poisoned water makes him delirious in Episode #16, "The Well"

CHAPTER EIGHT

Second Season Episodes

Episode number:	16
Episode title:	The Well
Original airdate:	9-27-73
Writer:	Kittridge Barton
Director:	Jerry Thorpe
Guest stars:	Tim McIntire, Hal Williams, Mae Mercer,
	TaRonce Allen, George Spell

THE TOWN of Crossroads and the surrounding countryside are hit by a drought. Approaching the town, Caine searches desperately for water. At last, a lone drifter offers him some. Caine drinks it—not knowing that it is poisoned. He falls into a delirium that convinces the inhabitants of Crossroads that he is a madman, an obvious threat to their community.

The sheriff tries to take Caine into custody but is roughly fended off by him; Caine, in his illness, doesn't know what he is doing. A young boy named Daniel witnesses the fight and takes Caine to be a hero. He hides Caine in his father's wagon and then smuggles him back to the modest homestead of his father, Caleb.

Caleb is an ex-slave, and it turns out he has water—in the form of a well—on his property; but, given his fear and distrust of the white community, he's not about to share his secret.

Caine's presence makes Caleb nervous, because he thinks the stranger may pose a threat to his secret. And, indeed, he does, for after an extensive search, the local deputy finds Caine at Caleb's ranch. Subsequently, the secret about the well comes out. The deputy is corrupt and pushes Caine into a fight by threatening Caleb. Caine knocks out the deputy with a single *kung-fu* move. This leaves Caleb to figure out what, if anything, he is going to do about his secret well.

Notes: Of this episode, David Carradine says, "There was a point at which I said, 'Look, we have to get some color in here. We have to.' So they wrote this one segment in." People liked the episode so much that a sequel was written for the third season (Episode #57, "The Last Raid").

John Furia says, "We thought there were unique parallels between a black man in the West and an Oriental man in the West—both of whom were outcasts because of the color of their skin and the prejudice that surrounded them; both of whom shared a unique sense of freedom." The episode emphasized the fact that even when a man "acquires" freedom, he isn't necessarily free. Part of this is because external prejudice still exists. Part of it has to do with self-perception, for, as Caine suggests, ultimately freedom can only come from within. At one point, Caine says to Caleb, "You look to others for your own freedom?"

Caleb responds, "Where else am I gonna find it?" Then, he stalks off.

Later, Caleb will more fully understand that freedom comes (as Furia notes) by "freeing yourself of anger, and by freeing yourself of your own prejudices and by, in a sense, acting free."

Furia's point was borne out explicitly in the episode—and also in some last-minute changes in the script. At the end of this episode, Daniel, Caleb's son, decides he wants to go with Caine. David Carradine explains, "In the script, Caine said, 'No, you stay with your father. He'll tell you exactly what to do.' And I said, 'No, that's not Caine.' I said, 'Why doesn't Caine just say yes and then let's see what happens.' And then we came up with a whole new response. The kid actually decides on his own that he should stay with his father—which I think is more in keeping with the philosophy."

Episode number:	**17**
Episode title:	**The Assassin**
Original airdate:	**10-4-73**
Writers:	**Spooner Glass, Daniel Ullman**

Director:	**Richard Lang**
Guest stars:	**Dana Elcar, James Keach,**
	William Glover, Robert Ito,
	Nobu McCarthy, Douglas V. Fowley,
	Beverly Kushida

Caine remembers Master Po's words: "Perfect wisdom is un-planned. Perfect living offers no guarantee of a peaceful death. . . . Learn first how to live. Learn second how not to kill. Learn third how to live with death. Learn fourth . . . how to die." The words serve as an epigraph for the episode, because, once again, Caine becomes embroiled in a deadly blood feud between two families of different heritages. Trading-post owner Swan and cargo shipper Noah are keeping apart Swan's half-Japanese daughter, Akido, and Noah's son, Abe. A wounding and a murder by a mysterious masked man only makes matters worse by increasing suspicions.

On learning that Swan's blacksmith is the mysterious masked man—as well as a *ninja*, or Japanese street-fighter, in disguise—Caine confronts him. The blacksmith attacks Caine, and the two men struggle, rolling into a river as they fight. Caine hurls the blacksmith off of him, and the blacksmith is accidentally killed when his head strikes a stone in the river. In the end, Caine encourages the two families to reconcile themselves before their loved ones are also hurt.

Notes: Guest star Robert Ito appeared in this episode, the *Kung Fu* pilot, and Episode #30 ("The Way of Violence Has No Mind").

Ito says that he played the role of the *ninja*, disguised as a blacksmith, before people knew what a *ninja* was. Jerry Thorpe, Ito reports, was no exception. Ito explains: "When we first started the episode, Jerry Thorpe—who was really a great man to work for—didn't know what a *ninja* was. They wanted a big man. And I said *ninja* aren't necessarily big. As a matter of fact, they are of all sizes. They could be fat, big, short, tall . . . it didn't make any difference. Their central ability was that they were able to mingle with whomever they were dealing with. If he knew a farmer, then he would know everything about farming. A priest? He knows everything about what a priest does. A blacksmith. A carpenter, whatever. The *ninja* is able to disguise himself. But his abilities are another matter. Those are things that he keeps to himself. And he doesn't display these *ninja* abilities until a crucial time.

"So when we began rehearsing for the segment, they had me dressed in a black hood, and my pants were too baggy. And then I explained that the man had to move. He had to have his pants tied to his legs so that he wouldn't trip on them. And then I explained that the type of mask that I would wear would be a long type of scarf. And I would wrap it around me so that it would be close to my head. And I could use it as a robe and other things besides just a hood. And it would also keep me from sucking in dust or whatever, if I had to crawl in small places. . . . This *ninja* was even able to dislocate his joints. So I gave him a limp to add to this part of his character."

In a scene that was subsequently cut from the final show, Ito says, his character temporarily dislocated his hip. This, Ito explains, is something that a *ninja* "really can do. You know, to get out of tight spots."

While this episode was action-oriented, it was also about love. In a flashback, Master Po says to the young Caine, "To know love, be like the running brook, which deaf, yet sings its melody for others to hear. Feel the pain of too much tenderness. Wake at dawn with a winged heart and give thanks for yet another day of loving."

Episode number:	**18**
Episode title:	**The Chalice**
Original airdate:	**10-11-73**
Writer:	**William Kelley**
Director:	**Jerry Thorpe**
Guest stars:	**Gilbert Roland, William Smith,**
	Lee Paul, Charles Dierkop,
	Pepe Serna, Victor Millan

In the desert of New Mexico, Padre Benito lies dying. He has been waylaid, shot and robbed of a gold chalice. Benito begs Caine to find the outlaws who stole the chalice from him . . . and adds that he would like Caine to take it back to the mission from which Benito stole it. It seems unlikely behavior for a priest, but when Caine gets to the mission he learns from Padre Braganza that Benito made the chalice with bits of gold that he had gathered over a period of twenty-six years. In conflict with his Franciscan vow of poverty, Benito had formed an attachment to his handiwork. When he left the monastery for another post, he could not bear to part with it.

This story puts Caine in mind of the attachment he once had for the shiny pebble that he finally snatched from his master's hand (in preparation for his departure from the Shaolin temple). After wanting that pebble in his hand for years, it was hard to part with it. A foolish want, Caine confessed to Master Kan. Kan responded, "Perhaps. The Universe contains a certain pebble known as The Earth. And many are the men who have formed attachments to it no less foolish than yours."

As Caine searches for Benito's goblet, he runs into troubles and endangers his life more than once. At last, however, he secures the goblet. Then, he goes to visit Padre Benito's grave. As he does, he thinks back to visiting Master Po's grave with Master Kan, and he thinks of Master Kan's eloquent eulogy: "May his bones find rest in this place. And may his passing, in its violence, not wake the tigers of outrage, the dragons of vengeance. May it rather, in its sadness, wake nothing but the dove in us, the lamb in others. So that together, in the bond of compassion, we may rejoice in the memory of Master Po . . . and wipe away forever the tears from the eyes of the blind lion." Caine listens, and before he turns to leave Po's grave, he takes a gold-hued pebble from the foot of the grave, puts it in his belt pouch, and walks away. Years later, he deposits this pebble at Benito's grave.

Notes: The script was originally titled "The Pebble." Under the title, the author typed these words: "Theme: That we are possessed by what we would possess; held in bondage to earth and vested things by the attachments we form for them—even so holy a thing as a chalice, so slight a thing as a pebble."

Episode number:	**19**
Episode title:	**The Brujo**
Original airdate:	**10-25-73**
Writers:	**Katharyn and Michael Michaelian**
Director:	**Richard Lang**
Guest stars:	**Benson Fong, Henry Darrow, Emilio Fernandez, Maria Elena Cordero, Rudolfo Hoyos, Felipe Turich**

The whole town of San Martin is fearful because its citizens are dying for no apparent reason. The people are convinced that their illness is the work of Carlos, a brujo, or male witch. The local priest has been unable to allay the town's fears, so Caine tries to help. He does this first by helping a baby recover from his mysterious malady. As soon as it is clear the baby is well, the baby's mother begs Caine to help break the witch's spell. "You have the power!" she cries at him. "I know it! I feel it!"

Caine tells the mother that the only power he has is his knowledge of himself, but still the mother insists that he use his knowledge to destroy Carlos. Carlos, whether his power is real or not, is, indeed, evil, and eventually Caine does have to confront him. When he does, he remembers Po's words about evil, about how one shouldn't let evil "pass through." Instead, one should reflect evil to its source. This is exactly what Caine does in a physical fight, when he turns Carlos's force back onto Carlos. In the end, Caine also tries to show the village how their fears made them, however unwillingly, complicitous in Carlos's evil rule.

Notes: Another of several episodes dealing with superstition and how it plays with men's minds. In the flashbacks, young Caine is fearful about a sorcerer's supposed curse. Master Po reminds Caine that "the undiscerning mind is like the root of a tree—it absorbs equally all that it touches— even the poison that would kill it."

Still, when a young boy dies, young Caine is convinced it is because of the curse.

YOUNG CAINE: Why is he dead, Master? I do not understand.
MASTER PO: Did not the boy believe he would die?
YOUNG CAINE: He would not believe otherwise.
MASTER PO: And so, his life had no choice but to fly away. Learn from him, Grasshopper—

Episode number:	**20**
Episode title:	**The Spirit Helper**
Original airdate:	**11-1-73**
Writer:	**John T. Dugan**
Director:	**Walter Doniger**

Guest stars:　　　　**Don Johnson, Bo Svenson,**
　　　　　　　　　　Scott Hylands, James A. Watson,
　　　　　　　　　　Khigh Dheigh, Rita Rogers

To learn the secrets of life and manhood, Nashebo, an Indian adolescent, prays endlessly to the "One Above" for assistance. In the midst of the young man's prayers, Caine strays from beneath a misty mountainside. The young man is convinced that he has found his spirit guide. Suddenly, screams and gunshots are heard; a Comanchero gang has killed Nashebo's father and kidnapped his mother, Crucita. Though Caine shuns Nashebo's worship of him, he agrees to help rescue the woman. After a near-successful attempt to do so, Nashebo and Caine are captured and tied to the ground.

Though Caine has already defeated the Comanchero gang's leader— Pike—in a fight, Pike challenges Caine again, in order to save face. Caine wins once more and is set free. Nashebo is untied, too, and he immediately aims to avenge his father's death by killing Pike. Nashebo lifts his machete to kill Pike, but Crucita and Caine try to stop him. Caine says, "Is it not better to embrace the living than avenge the dead?" Nashebo must think that it is, for he hurls his machete away and runs into his mother's arms.

Notes: Don Johnson, later a star on the TV series *Miami Vice*, played Nashebo—one of Johnson's first major roles in Hollywood.

David Carradine remembers suggesting Johnson for the part: "I said, 'He's got star quality. He's going to be big.'" Johnson never forgot the recommendation, and, years later, he cast Carradine to play his father in a music video.

Episode number:	**21**
Episode title:	**The Squaw Man**
Original airdate:	**11-8-73**
Writer:	**Arthur Dales**
Director:	**John Llewellyn Moxey**
Guest stars:	**Jack Elam, Logan Ramsey,**
	Elliott Street, Rosana Soto,
	Rex Holman, Booth Colman,
	Eddie Firestone, James Hong, Victor-Sen Yung

Lin (James Hong) roasting a stolen pig that he has no intention of sharing with his fellow beggars in Episode #21, "The Squaw Man"

Caine hooks up with a poor farmer named Marcus Taylor and his pregnant Indian wife, Kiona. The three journey with a dead man's body into a lawless town. Marcus explains that he shot the man when he tried to make off with his horse. The townspeople (out of sheer prejudice, since Marcus is travelling with a half-Chinese and an Indian) decide to hang Marcus and Caine, but then someone identifies the dead man as an outlaw—the son of the famous bandit Sam Blake. Marcus is an instant hero. Everyone shakes his hand and buys him drinks.

The praise quickly goes to Marcus's head. Hoping for more approval, Marcus decides to go out and find Blake and kill him, too. Caine, worried that Marcus will get himself killed, goes along to protect him. During his hunt, Marcus accidentally wounds a US Marshal. Caine tends to the marshal's wounds while Marcus, undeterred by his error, keeps looking for Blake.

Meanwhile, Blake hears about his son's death and comes looking to avenge the killing. Marcus—frustrated by what he perceives as Caine's cowardice—has ordered Caine to stay away from him. Caine keeps his distance, but when he hears gunshots, he comes back to save Marcus from Blake.

In the end, Marcus brings the outlaws into town, but he decides he doesn't want any reward for capturing the men.

Notes: James Hong recalls this episode as one of his favorites. He remembers it in particular because his character—a scraggly old man named Lin—was a bit different from the ones he normally played. In the flashback scenes in China, Lin steals a pig, roasts it, and is unwilling to share it with the hungry. Like Marcus, the character of Lin has allowed his financial poverty to make his spirit penurious as well. In the foreground story, Marcus gets a chance to learn to appreciate the gift of his Indian wife's love. In the flashbacks, however, the old man Lin is shot before he ever gets a chance to learn such a lesson.

Episode number:	22
Episode title:	The Salamander
Original airdate:	11-15-73
Writer:	Del Reisman
Director:	Richard Lang
Guest stars:	David Huddleston, Ed Flanders, Ramon Bieri, James Lee Reeves

Caine tries to help Andy, a suicidal man who is uncertain about his ability to distinguish fantasy from reality. Caine leads Andy to Alonzo, his long-lost father. (Alonzo's wife, Andy's mother, went mad years ago.) Alonzo, and his partner, John Bates, are working in a dried-up mine in a virtual ghost town. Andy remains confused about his perceptions. He keeps on thinking he sees Bates spying on him. When he sits by a fire, he decides that the flames are imaginary, that they are only happening in his head. Andy's despair increases.

When Alonzo finally thinks he's "struck gold," his partner causes a fire that traps Alonzo, Andy, and Caine in the mine. It turns out Andy's visions of the sneaky Bates were not visions at all.

After Caine guides Andy to safety, Bates shoots and kills Alonzo. Bates tries to shoot Andy as well, but Caine kicks Bates's gun out of his hand. Bates, hoping to kill Andy with his bare hands, rushes at the confused man. Andy instinctively drops to the ground to protect himself, and Bates plunges past him into the fire. The mine shaft collapses and buries Bates.

Andy finally is able to trust his perceptions as real. Unburdened of his fears about going mad, Andy is able to choose to live.

Notes: The following discussion between Andy and Caine helps explain the title of this episode.

CAINE: As a child I read of the salamander. A strange beast. He did not know what was to become of him. He was ugly. . . . And some men threw him into the fire to die. But the flame did not destroy him. It tested him . . . and made him stronger.

ANDY: Was he still . . . ugly?

CAINE: I do not know how the salamander saw . . . *himself.*

Episode number:	23
Episode title:	**The *Tong***
Original airdate:	**11-29-73**
Writer:	**Robert Schlitt**
Director:	**Robert Totten**
Guest stars:	**Diana Douglas, Richard Loo, Tad Horino, Kinjo Shibuya, Carey Wong**

Caine bands together with an evangelist, Sister Richardson, to shelter a boy named Wing from Chen, his slave master. Chen is a Chinese underworld lord living in America. When Chen learns that Caine is a Shaolin, he tries to kill him (on the instruction of Li, the leader of Chen's *tong*—a Chinese association or clan). Chen hurls a hatchet at Caine's back, and Caine whirls around and catches it. Wing is amazed. He thinks his protector is magical. Li, on the other hand, is even more worried: if other people know of this Shaolin's power, they may try to follow him, rather than follow the leader of the *tong*. Li tells Caine he will have to fight Ah Quong, the *tong*'s executioner. But even Ah Quong is afraid of Caine. He's not too afraid, however, to order his henchman to shoot a silver-tipped arrow at Caine. The henchman does this, and Caine is impaled, yet he still appears healthy. Caine breaks off the tip of arrow in his chest and pulls the arrow's shaft from his back. He hands the bits of the arrow to Ah Quong, who immediately loses his nerve and flees. Then Caine collapses. Wing and Sister Richardson stay to nurse him back to health. Before Caine leaves he tells Sister Richardson that if she does not save Wing's soul, she will at least have helped to set his soul free.

Notes: Robert Schlitt, the writer of this episode, points out that in the end, Caine effectively "psychs his opponent out." After he is hit by the arrow, Caine is quite seriously wounded. He is, in fact, near death. Of course, since he is human, he is unable to fight, but the myth of Caine is so strong that it saves him. Ultimately, Schlitt says, "it was up to the audience as to whether . . . to believe Caine had been damaged or was really invulnerable. But it was also up to [Caine's opponent] to believe that."

The idea for the show—particularly for the scene in which Caine catches the hatchet—came, Schlitt says, from Archie Moore, the boxer. Apparently once, when Moore was older, reporters were asking him about whether he was too old to fight. While they were asking, a fly came buzzing into the room they were in. A reporter said something about how a person's reflexes go when they age. Then, as Robert Schlitt reports it, "Archie Moore reached out and grabbed this fly and held it in his hand and said, 'Yeah, I suppose you're right. After a while, your reflexes are just shot,' and he opens the hand and lets the fly go." Schlitt goes on to say that Archie Moore "worked by a kind of psych-out. And so I got the idea that Caine's ultimate way of not having to fight would be to invoke this magical power that he was usually trying to hide."

Diana Douglas, who played Sister Richardson in this episode, is the mother of actor Michael Douglas and the former wife of Kirk Douglas, the veteran Hollywood leading man.

Episode number:	**24**
Episode title:	**The Soldier**
Original airdate:	**12-6-73**
Story:	**Calvin Clements, Jr.**
Teleplay:	**Ed Waters**
Director:	**Richard Lang**
Guest stars:	**Tim Matheson, Myron Healey, John Dennis, Douglas Dirkson, Margaret Fairchild, Frank Whiteman, Skip Riley**

Caine contemplates the aftermath of a battle. In front of him, a dozen cavalrymen and almost as many *bandoleros* (roving marauders) lie sprawled on the ground. As he observes the carnage, Caine sees one man—Lieutenant Wyland—purposely shoot himself in the thigh (to hide his cowardice in battle). When the army arrives on the scene, they mistake Caine for one of the *bandoleros* and arrest him.

Caine is jailed with two other soldiers, Graf and Hamel, incarcerated for their malingering. All three men break jail, and Wyland and his men pursue them. Caine breaks free, and Wyland chases after him. Finally, Wyland catches up. When he meets Caine eye-to-eye, however, Wyland cannot shoot. He is shamed, once again, by his own cowardice. As Wyland talks with Caine about why he cannot "do his duty" and be a soldier who shoots men, the real *bandoleros* return. In defending Caine, Wyland takes a bullet in the shoulder. Caine points out that any man who cannot kill but is willing to risk his life for another is no coward. No longer ashamed, Wyland decides that perhaps his problem is not that he is a coward but that he is in the wrong line of work.

Notes: In a flashback scene, the disciple Caine shows off his skills in front of several novices. He blindfolds himself and has four young students try to attack him with various weapons. Kan sees this and hurries over to Caine and the novices. When Caine proudly removes his blindfold, he doesn't find four impressed novices but Master Kan's dour face. The scene continues:

MASTER KAN: Had you good cause to risk this danger?
DISCIPLE CAINE: My purpose was to prove my agility, Master . . . and my courage.
MASTER KAN: I had hopes such qualities were already yours.
DISCIPLE CAINE: I sought to test them, Master.
MASTER KAN: For yourself or . . . for them? Is it not better to see yourself truly than to care how others see you?

Episode number:	25
Episode title:	**The Hoots**
Original airdate:	**12-13-73**
Story:	**Jason McKinnon**
Teleplay:	**Lionel E. Siegel**
Director:	**Robert Totten**
Guest stars:	**Howard da Silva, Anthony Zerbe, Laurie Prange, Jock Mahoney, Rance Howard**

After Caine helps heal a woman named Gretchen, he becomes involved with the Hutterite religious order to which she belongs. The sheep-herding Hutterites—members of a branch of the Anabaptist Christian church that emigrated to the American West to escape religious intolerance in Russia—find themselves in a conflict with a group of local cattlemen. Because the Hutterites' sheep are sickly, the cattlemen have cut off the animals' access to the local water hole. The sheep aren't contagious, but the pacifist Hutterites accept this injustice, rather than risk violence. Otto Schultz, the leader of the group, tells Caine that he wants to avoid not only sin, but anything that will tempt men to sin. Later, another member of the religious order will explain to Caine that "Otto does not believe that life is meant to be enjoyed. It's work. Not play." These harsh words make Caine remember Master Kan's words: "The purpose of discipline is to live more fully, not less."

Not long after, one of the Hutterites tries to negotiate with the cattle herders. They respond to his efforts by shaving off his beard—a sacred mark of his order. Then, a cow dies. The cattlemen immediately interpret the animal's death to be a result of the sheep disease and attack the Hutterite settlement to kill the flock and burn the buildings. Caine helps defend the Hutterites, and even Schultz raises a hand to defend himself. He is acting on Caine's dictum that if a man of peace is attacked with a stick, he may take the stick away.

Notes: This is one of the episodes in which Caine gets to play his flute. He has, too, another one of his conversations in which it is clear that his "faith," his religion, is life. As such, his beliefs are well within the Judeo-Christian tradition (as long as that tradition is read rather liberally). All this can be seen in the conversation that Caine has with Gretchen, who has heard, for the first time, the lovely sound of the flute.

GRETCHEN: What was that?
CAINE: A flute. . . . Have you never heard one before?
GRETCHEN: (*shakes her head no*)
CAINE: The sound is beautiful to me.
GRETCHEN: Otto Schultz says . . . things like that are frivolous and waste time. They make you lazy.
CAINE: This is part of your religion?
GRETCHEN: It's what Otto Schultz says. But I haven't found it in the Bible. Our ways are based on the Book of Acts, chapter two, verses forty-four and forty-five . . . 'all that believed were together and had all things common.'
CAINE: That is a beautiful way to live.
GRETCHEN: Do you know the Bible?

CAINE: I have read it . . . Is it not filled with beauty? Songs of sadness and also joy?

Episode number:	26
Episode title:	**The Elixir**
Original airdate:	**12-20-73**
Writer:	**A. Martin Zweiback**
Director:	**Walter Doniger**
Guest stars:	**Diana Muldaur, David Canary,**
	Matt Clark, Walter Barnes,
	Richard Caine, Don Megowan

Caine saves Niebo, a hunchback, from three town roughs; then he rides off in a medicine-show wagon with Niebo and Theodora, a beautiful peddler of "cure-all" potions. It turns out that Theodora is being trailed by gunman Frank Grogan, who wants to kill her for deserting him. Strong-willed and independent, Theodora says she is slave to no man, though she does make advances to Caine. Niebo is infuriated by her behavior. Out for vengeance, he finds Grogan and promises to lead him to Theodora. When they reach camp, Niebo pulls a knife, and Grogan shoots it out of his hand. Caine hears the shot and arrives with Theodora. Caine knocks Grogan unconscious, but not before the gunman wounds Niebo. Theodora becomes instantly hysterical. "I don't want to be all alone," she weeps. When Niebo recovers, she humbly confesses her affection for him, and with the help of Caine, she understands that freedom, without love and service, is emptiness.

Notes: Caine teaches many of the people he encounters that true freedom is intentional. It does not mean roaming through life aimlessly. Clearly, this is something Caine is well aware of since his own life has become a continuous search for his half-brother; and yet this search does not obviate his desire to help the people he meets on his way.

Episode number:	27
Episode title:	**The Gunman**
Original airdate:	**1-3-74**
Writer:	**Robert Newin**
Director:	**Richard Lang**

Guest stars: **Andy Prine, Katharine Woodville,
                   Jack Riley, Sandy Kenyon,
                   Alan Fudge**

Caine brings a wounded gunslinger named White to the cabin of
the young widow Nedra Chamberlain. It turns out the two have
met before. Indeed, years earlier, White saw Nedra's husband beat-
ing her, so he killed him.

As Caine learns more about White's background, he thinks
back to Master Kan's advice: "If one intervenes one is swimming
upstream, against the flow of life. Sometimes that seems called for.
Right action can come only from inner conviction. But there is
nothing written which guarantees that that which comes from a
good motive will bring good results. Intervention is therefore its
own paradox."

As Nedra nurses White back to health, their old romance is re-
kindled, only to be snuffed out when Nedra is assaulted by a
townsman—whom White subsequently kills. En route to town,
with the body of the townsman, Caine and Nedra are arrested, because they refuse to tell the sheriff where White can be found.
Meanwhile, White flees a vigilante group made up of the dead
townsman's friends. The vigilantes free Nedra and Caine from jail,
but only so they can lynch them. Caine single-handedly dispenses
with the vigilante group, while Nedra goes to White's hiding place.

Eventually, White is gunned down. Nedra's love is lost once
more, this time for good. She feels even lonelier than she ever did
before, but Caine tells her, "Does not tomorrow begin now?"

Notes: In the climactic scene, White and the sheriff have guns trained on
each other. White has the advantage, but he drops his gun arm—just at the
point at which another man might have shot. Just then, a third man,
Royal—who has taken cover nearby— shoots and kills White. Nedra
screams hysterically, throws herself on White, and begs him not to die.
Then, this conversation takes place:

SHERIFF: (*to Royal*) You murdered him.
ROYAL: (*coolly*) He was wanted dead or alive . . . Just doin' my job.
SHERIFF: He had me. Why didn't he shoot?
CAINE: He lost his 'edge.' He did not see 'enemy.' He saw you. A
man.

Episode number:	**28**
Episode title:	**Empty Pages of a Dead Book**
Original airdate:	**1-10-74**
Writer:	**Charles A. McDaniel**
Director:	**John Llewellyn Moxey**
Guest stars:	**Robert Foxworth, Slim Pickens,**
	Doreen Lang, Bruce Carradine,
	Nate Esformes, Carlos Romero

Caine camps with Bart Fisher, a member of the criminal Fisher gang. In rides young Texas Ranger McNelly, dedicated to finding each of the Fishers, whose names appear in a book McNelly's late ranger father left behind. McNelly shoots Bart Fisher in the arm.

In court for the wounding of Bart Fisher, McNelly learns that the Fishers have been granted amnesty, and they are living as peaceful citizens of the state. The judge has no choice but to relieve McNelly of his badge.

Outside the court, Bart's brother Joe Billy and three other Fishers ambush McNelly. Caine steps in to assist the ranger. During the fight, Joe Billy is killed while trying to reach for a gun on a balcony. Back in court, the Fishers testify that Caine and McNelly threw their brother off the balcony.

Caine and McNelly are convicted of murder and imprisoned. They break jail. The sheriff comes after them and is thrown from his horse and badly injured. Rather than leave him to die, McNelly and Caine take the lawman to town and, then, surrender. The judge, now believing they were framed, frees the men. This leaves McNelly confused about the injustices that can be wrought by due process of the law. McNelly gives the judge his book of wanted men, so the book can be buried with Joe Billy.

Notes: One of the significant flashbacks in this episode involves a definition of the purpose of the law.

YOUNG CAINE: Master, must I always serve the law?

MASTER KAN: Hear the law; *serve* justice.

YOUNG CAINE: I have seen a law broken . . . Do I serve justice if I let it go unpunished?

MASTER KAN: What is the purpose of the law?

YOUNG CAINE: *(thinking about it)* Discipline.

MASTER KAN: And who is served by this discipline?
(Still troubled, the young Caine moves a bit away.)
YOUNG CAINE: Each one who obeys the law.
MASTER KAN: Then to break *that* law denies justice only to one's self.
YOUNG CAINE: *(a beat)* It is the same with all laws? If I break them, do I deny justice only to myself?
MASTER KAN: *(studies the boy a beat)* What is the purpose of the law?
(The boy frowns, not certain of the Master's meaning. Kan turns, moves slowly away.)

Also, guest star Bruce Carradine is David Carradine's (Caine's) brother.

Episode number:	**29**
Episode title:	**A Dream Within a Dream**
Original airdate:	**1-17-74**
Writer:	**John T. Dugan**
Director:	**Richard Lang**
Guest stars:	**John Drew Barrymore, Ruth Roman, Tina Louise, Sorrell Booke, Howard Duff, Mark Miller**

Caine sees Jason Norman hanging from a tree. Although Caine soon learns that many people had a motive to kill him, everyone he meets denies the report of his death. Denying their own feelings, they claim that Norman was too rich, powerful, and self-confident to have had enemies.

When Caine returns to the scene of the hanging, he finds the body gone. Then, the sheriff's henchmen attack Caine. Caine overcomes them with *kung-fu*, and, as he does, he finds a watch. Later, Mrs. Norman identifies the watch as belonging to her husband. Now the sheriff—willing to admit the man is dead—accuses Caine of killing Norman, robbing him, and burying his body in quicksand. But, finally, McGregor, a sculptor of gravestones, comes foreword and admits that he saw Norman hang himself, that he buried the body to cover up the suicide. Everyone is shocked that such a man could have killed himself. Each of them—despite both their hate and admiration for Norman—is left feeling diminished by the death. Caine tells them, "He is not dead. He will always be here—till each of you buries him."

Notes: A philosophical flashback scene tries to define "man," as follows:

YOUNG CAINE: What is the truth of *man*, Master?
MASTER KAN: It has been said that a man is three things: What he thinks he is; what others think he is; and what he really is. Which of these do you believe to be the truth?
YOUNG CAINE: What a man really is. But if he is in error about himself, and others are also wrong . . . who is there left to say *what* he really is?
MASTER KAN: Excellent, my son. And to this sum add another question: At what point in time can a man be fixed and frozen . . . if he is to live and grow?

Episode number:	**30**
Episode title:	**The Way of Violence Has No Mind**
Original airdate:	**1-24-74**
Writer:	**David Michael Korn**
Director:	**Lee Philips**
Guest stars:	**Gary Merrill, Ron Soble,**
	Fritz Weaver, Robert Ito,
	Victor-Sen Yung, Ted Gehring,
	William Traylor

The story opens with Caine being mistaken for an agent of a Chinese bandit—Captain Lee—who has been robbing whites and giving money to persecuted Chinese. The person who mistakes Caine is a mine owner named Hillquist. Captain Lee comes to Caine's rescue—and takes the opportunity to steal some gold from Hillquist. With Lee are his cohorts Chu and the young boy Quoy. Lee, Chu, and Quoy are all amazed when Caine refuses Lee's offer of gold.

Caine trudges off and meets a farmer, Dan Hoyle, and his wife. Hillquist comes looking for Lee and finds Caine. He ties Caine to a wheel and dunks him in a stream. Again, Lee comes to Caine's aid and drives Hillquist away. In the process, Hoyle is wounded. Caine tends to Hoyle's injury, as well as to the injuries of some wounded baby chicks. Quoy wonders at Caine's compassion. Leé laughs at Caine but is still touched by him.

Hillquist returns with more men and attacks the farmhouse. Lee and Chu fire back, but Quoy, influenced by Caine, does not use his gun. Lee and Chu run out of ammunition when the sheriff arrives with a posse. The sheriff captures Hillquist and demands that the Chinese bandit surrender. Lee says he will surrender, but he reaches for Quoy's gun—clearly he means to shoot his way out of the situation. Caine stops Lee, reminding him that he gave his word. The two men fight. During the brawl, Lee tosses his gun to Chu. This leaves Chu with the choice of giving himself up or escaping out the back. Chu surrenders.

Once the sheriff has both Lee and Chu in custody, he says to them, "You took a lot of money but you never killed. I'll speak up for you."

Notes: The title of this episode comes from a flashback with Master Kan.

MASTER KAN: What is gained by using one's strength in violence and anger?
YOUNG CAINE: A victory that is swift.
MASTER KAN: Yet to be violent is to be weak, for violence has no mind. Is it not wiser to seek a man's love than to desire his swift defeat?

The shooting schedule for this episode, which was at that point titled "The Raiders," is reproduced as an appendix to this book.

Episode number:	**31**
Episode title:	**In Uncertain Bondage**
Original airdate:	**2-7-74**
Writers:	**Abe Polsky, Ed Waters**
Director:	**Richard Lang**
Guest stars:	**Warren Vanders, Judy Pace,**
	Lynda Day George, Roger Mosely

Dora, an aristocratic southern belle, is in a carriage en route to her doctor. She has a heart seizure on the way. Passerby Caine stops to help her and is taken along. Suddenly the carriage swerves into a quarry. The driver, Tait, his black servant, Seth, and Dora's black maid, Jenny, are kidnapping Dora. When Caine comes to Dora's defense, he is wounded by gunshot and thrown, with Dora, into a pit. The kidnappers want Dora to write a ransom note to her father, but Dora refuses.

Then, upon learning that Tait plans to kill Dora after the ransom money is delivered, Jenny decides she is no longer willing to go along with the kidnapping. For her rebellion, she, too, is thrown into the pit. Not long after, Seth rebels and is thrown into the pit as well.

In the pit, Caine fashions a line with laces from Dora's dress. The group escapes, only to be confronted with Tait and a sword. Using *kung-fu*, Caine disarms and captures Tait. Before Caine leaves, Dora thanks him for teaching her that there is no less dignity in serving others than in being served.

Notes: This is one of the episodes which features interlocking flashbacks—continuous scenes from Caine's past that are shown chronologically through the hour-long episode. This segment's flashbacks focus on the master-disciple relationship between Kan and Caine. In them, the two examine what it means to serve and be served.

Episode number:	**32**
Episode title:	**Night of the Owls, Day of the Doves**
Original airdate:	**2-14-74**
Story:	**Frank Dandridge, Ed Waters**
Teleplay:	**Ed Waters**
Director:	**John Llewellyn Moxey**
Guest stars:	**Barry Atwater, Ken Swofford,**
	Anne Francis, Rayford Barnes,
	Arlene Farber, Juno Dawson,
	Paul Harper, Claire Nono

Farmer Sam Wallace dies, but not before he gives his will to Caine. In it, Wallace leaves everything he has to a group of prostitutes. This is a considerable amount of money, mostly because Sam's land was valuable. Knowing about the will, a group of vigilantes—called the Owls and led by a man named Thurmond—come to the brothel and try to take the will by force. With a series of deft *kung-fu* moves, Caine sends the vigilantes flying out a window. The group retreats, but Thurmond threatens more violent measures and even tells the sheriff not to interfere. The sheriff responds obediently and leaves town.

Since he is not interested in material wealth, Caine tells the prostitutes that perhaps they should surrender the will to save themselves trouble. This advice particularly disgusts a Chinese harlot named Cinnamon. She says to Caine, "A Shaolin is only important to himself." Caine understands the judgment in her words, but when he asks her what she wants of him, she says she wants nothing.

Later, Caine returns to the brothel to save the women from the Owls—who have besieged the house. Caine is able to dispose of all the vigilantes save for Thurmond. Just then the sheriff shows up with a posse of US marshals. Thurmond is hauled away, and the girls are left with an inheritance—and the chance for a new way of life.

Notes: Cinnamon is clearly bitter about Caine's failure to defend the brothel. In this episode, she tries to bait him by saying, "I was told a Shaolin didn't know fear."

Caine tells her what he has been told: "The greatest victor wins without a battle. Yield and you need not break."

Cinnamon remains unconvinced, but then Caine discovers why. She says that she was sold so that her cousin could go to study at the Shaolin temple. Caine assures her that the Shaolin masters did not know this, for if they did they "would have felt a duty to undo the harm."

Cinnamon still seems unmoved. Certainly the treatment of women within the Chinese culture has not led her to believe that any Chinese man—Shaolin or not—values a woman and a man's life equally.

Episode number:	**33**
Episode title:	**Crossties**
Original airdate:	**2-21-74**
Writer:	**Robert Schlitt**
Director:	**Richard Lang**
Guest stars:	**Barry Sullivan, John Anderson, Denver Pyle, Harrison Ford, Andy Robinson, Dennis Fimple**

Caine is caught in a conflict between the Youngblood gang (a group of ex-farmers struggling against the interests of the railroad—

Once Caine's fellow student at the Shaolin temple, Chen Yi (Soon-Teck Oh) shows up in the American West—as does the wooden ant he once carved—in Episode #34, "The Passion of Chen Yi."

which pushed them off their land) and Edwards, a private detective who wants to destroy the Youngbloods.

The railroad, tired of the struggle—and of Edwards's tactics—offers amnesty to the Youngbloods and promises to submit their claims to arbitration. It turns out, however, that Edwards is trying to trap the Youngbloods by luring them into negotiation and then killing them. When Edwards pulls his gun on the Youngbloods, Caine kicks it out of his hand and reasons with Edwards's henchmen to surrender. Edwards orders his men to shoot, and, when they don't, Edwards, maddened by hate, falls sobbing to his knees. At this spectacle, Edwards's men lower their guns. With peace at hand, the Youngbloods look forward to plowing their land again.

Notes: Writer Robert Schlitt explains the origin of this show: while looking at a Warners Bros. property list, he found that somewhere on the back lot there was a mint-condition 1880 steam locomotive, a caboose, two railroad cars, and two hundred feet of track. "So," Schlitt says, "we thought, 'Great. Let's do a train story.' And so I wrote a story about the James boys versus the Pinkertons, and it was kind of my take on Vietnam. The reason the war was going to end was simply because it was inefficient, wasteful. It wasn't going to be decided as a matter of principle, on who were the good guys and who were the bad guys. . . .

"[In the episode, you had these men who] were thrown off the land by the railroad, and they vowed to fight to the death to keep the land. And then you had Pinkerton, who was going to civilize the West, and he vowed to fight to the death to destroy these outlaws. And this was going on and on, and the outlaws would win one, and the Pinkertons would win one. And then some guy from the home office in Chicago asks, 'How much are these bandits costing us, and how much is it costing us to keep these Pinkertons out there fighting?'"

Eventually the solution came from the outside, from people who weren't interested in morality, but simply in ending the conflict. "And," Schlitt continues, "the people who were in this war just got so accustomed to fighting it, they couldn't allow themselves to let it end on anything but a moral basis."

A funny detail: when Schlitt and others finally went to the back lot to look at the train that prompted the episode, it turned out to be three-quarter scale, because it was designed to be used for background shots only. "When you stood next to it, you would be as tall as the engine," Schlitt recalls. "This was a little bit awkward, so what we finally had to do was build trenches around the front of the train for the close-ups. That way when the actors stood next to it, they would be proper height."

Episode number:	**34**
Episode title:	**The Passion of Chen Yi**
Original airdate:	**2-28-74**
Writer:	**John T. Dugan**
Director:	**John Llewellyn Moxey**
Guest stars:	**Bethel Leslie, Mariana Hill,**
	Robert Middleton, Soon-Teck Oh,
	Arch Johnson, Ivor Francis

Caine thinks about Chen Yi, a young man who was expelled from the Shaolin temple because he was an unsuccessful disciple. Before Chen Yi left, he had an odd interchange with Caine in which he gave Caine a carved wooden ant. Chen Yi was a talented artisan, but the gift was meant to be demeaning. Recognizing the insult, Caine had refused the gift, but Chen Yi had challenged him to a fight. Caine lost, and, as a result, had to follow custom and accept Chen Yi's gift.

Now, in the West, Caine senses his old colleague is near, and he goes to find him. It turns out Chen Yi is in jail and soon to be hanged for killing a man named Dan Rodden. Unable to visit the prisoner, Caine gets himself thrown in jail so he can learn what happened. It turns out that Chen is in love with a woman named Louise. Caine is told that Chen Yi killed Rodden after he found Rodden with Louise. Chen is prepared to die: he is unwilling to accept help from Caine and he has already willed his valuable collection of carvings to Louise.

Uneasy with the details of the story, Caine breaks jail and goes to visit Louise and Rita, her wheelchair-bound sister. On his approach to their shack, Caine is certain he hears two sets of footsteps inside the house.

Shortly after, Caine is recaptured. Back in jail, he tries to convince Chen that he may be misperceiving the woman he loves. Chen remains unconvinced. In order to save Chen, Caine challenges him to a fight; Caine knows that if he wins, Chen will be obliged to do Caine's bidding. Caine does win the contest, and he says that what he wants Chen to do is to escape jail and go to the sisters' shack. Unable to refuse, Chen does this with Caine.

When the two men reach the shack, Louise seems less than happy to see Chen. Soon, it is revealed that in fact it was Rita who killed Rodden and made it appear that Louise was the murderer. Chen, out of love, offered to take the blame. Confronted with this information, Rita jumps up out of her wheelchair and seizes a gun—just as a US marshal arrives to see her standing on her supposedly useless legs. Caine and Chen go free, but not before Caine gives Chen a gift—the wooden ant from years ago.

Notes: In order to get thrown into jail with Chen Yi, Caine decides to rob a bank. He enters the bank, bows to the teller, and then says, "Please . . . I wish your money." The teller asks if he has an account at the bank. "I do not," Caine says, "I propose to rob your bank." The teller is shocked and Caine assures her, "Not *all* your money. Just . . . whatever is customary in such cases."

Actor Soon-Teck Oh, who played Chen Yi in this episode, remembers being particularly impressed by the fact that the story included an interracial romance. Certainly, the relationship wasn't a happy one, but, says the actor, "A relationship of some kind was acknowledged. And I thought that was something else."

Episode number:	35
Episode title:	**The Arrogant Dragon**
Original airdate:	**3-14-74**
Story:	**Barbara Melzer, Katharyn and Michael Michaelian**
Director:	**Richard Lang**
Guest stars:	**Richard Loo, Jocelyne Lew,**
	Edward Walsh, Dalton Leong,
	James Hong, Yuki Shimoda

Aging Wu Chang is secretly planning to take his daughter Kem back to China and retire, even though this represents a violation of his oath never to leave the *tong*, the Chinese association, that he heads. His secretary, Men Han, betrays him and reveals his plans. As a result, the *tong* tribunal sentences him to die.

Then, Caine brings Kem word that his friend and her lover, Li Tom, is dead. Knowing Caine is a Shaolin, Kem begs him to save her father. He refuses since he is unable to interfere in matters of honor. Later, however, when she offers to sleep with him, he learns she is pregnant by Li Tom, and he decides to help her father anyway.

His decision comes just in time, for if Wu does not take his own life by sunset, the *tong*'s executioner will kill him. In thinking about how he can help, Caine remembers a special potion that Master Kan told him about years ago: "Mixed with the white of an egg, it is effective for the relieving of pain in bruises and swelling. Taken internally, it quiets the heart and lungs—or causes death."

A small amount of the herb can quiet the heart and lung, without causing death, though it is difficult to determine how much will produce the appearance of death (that is, no heartbeat, no breathing) without actually killing a person. Given Wu's desperate situation, Caine takes the risk, gives Wu the herb, and effectively helps Wu simulate his own death. At first, the tong is deceived, but after the funeral, a suspicious member discovers the truth. Invoking that part of the tong code which allows a condemned man to appoint a champion, Caine battles the executioner and wins.

Notes: The morality of this episode is potentially problematic since Caine helps a man to disavow his own word. The final lines of the episode, in a flashback, resolve the apparent contradiction. Caine asks Master Po what is the "greatest obligation" that we have. Po responds, "To live, Grasshopper. To live!"

Episode number:	**36**
Episode title:	**The Nature of Evil**
Original airdate:	**3-21-74**
Writer:	**Gerald Sanford**
Director:	**Robert M. Lewis**
Guest stars:	**Morgan Woodward, Shelly Novak, John Carradine, Barbara Colby, Kelly Thordsen, James Gammon, Robert Donley**

Caine comes to Ninevah, a town incapacitated by a mysterious terror. Here, Caine finds his old friend, the Reverend Serenity Johnson (from Episode #2), who is looking for the killer of Sonny Jim, the mute man who had been Serenity's assistant and, since Serenity's blinding, his "eyes." Bascomb, a bounty hunter, is also seeking this otherwise nameless adversary. Finally, Bascomb finds him in a shadowy hotel room, but he can't quite see him. Instead, he hears a voice that says, "You don't want me." Then, a "Wanted" poster for Caine is dropped at Bascomb's feet.

Bascomb confronts Caine, who disarms him at a corral. Bascomb opens the corral gate to retrieve his gun, which is lying just beyond the fence, and is trampled by horses.

Finally, in a soap factory, Caine comes face-to-face with "the Adversary." The Adversary asks him why he has come. Caine says, "All men have run from you in fear. Someone must face you." A fierce battle ensues, a fire breaks out, and the evil man falls into a burning caldron.

Notes: In a flashback, the young Caine confesses to Po that he has been disturbed by the evil he sees within himself. Po tries to help Caine understand the nature of evil.

MASTER PO: Do you sometimes love, Grasshopper, feel joy? Do you sometimes take pride in what you have accomplished?

YOUNG CAINE: Often, Master!
MASTER PO: And do you sometimes feel Good?
YOUNG CAINE: I try.
MASTER PO: But the threads that make up our human nature are two-ended. There is no capacity for feeling pride without an equal capacity for feeling shame. One cannot feel joy unless one can also feel despair. We have no capacity for good without an equal capacity for evil.

Episode number:	**37**
Episode title:	**The Cenotaph, Part 1**
Original airdate:	**4-4-74**
Writer:	**William Kelley**
Director:	**Richard Lang**
Guest stars:	**Stefan Gierasch, Michael Pataki,**
	Robert Ridgley, Nancy Kwan,
	Ned Romero, Ed Bakey,
	Ivan Naranjo

Caine meets up with a madman named McBurney. McBurney hijacks a stagecoach (which happens to be transporting some gold) in order to carry his dying wife to her Indian people. Because he accidentally stumbles on the stagecoach, Caine goes along.

The incident makes him think of a time right after he was graduated from the Shaolin temple. He remembers how, back in China, he found an abandoned sedan chair . . . and close by, Mayli Ho, the emperor's concubine.

She tells him that she has been ravished by Kai Tong, a warlord looking for her routed attendants and then—she suspects—coming back to kidnap her.

Caine does not understand completely what has happened to her, for he does not know what "being ravished" means. He tells Mayli, "I knew its meaning . . . but nothing of its practice." Mayli finds this incredible. "It may seem so," Caine says, "but our masters are practical men. If a thing is not likely to improve one's priesthood, it is not discussed." Then, he says, in utter seriousness,

The crazy McBurney (Stefan Giersach) takes the reins as Caine journeys to a sacred Sioux burial ground, in Episode #37, "The Cenotaph, Part 1."

"As a practical matter, Shaolin priests have very little to do with being ravished. . . ."

Not long after, Kai returns and battles Caine, who wins and goes off with Mayli.

In the foreground story, in the American West, the hijacked coach arrives at a cabin. Here, McBurney shows Caine a huge box—in which, he says, the dying Anna lies. After a few run-ins with outlaws and Indians, McBurney is wounded. As a priest, Caine says he'll marry McBurney and Anna.

Then, Caine thinks back to China. He remembers Mayli questioning him about his feelings.

MAYLI: Do you love me, Kwai Chang?
CAINE: I . . . do not know.
MAYLI: Could you learn to love me?
CAINE: I . . . do not know.

She asks him if love is forbidden to him. He tells her that it is not, but that since marriage is forbidden, love is not practical for him. He asks her if love is forbidden to her. She says she's not sure, but since marriage is forbidden to concubines, love is not practical for her.

Notes: In this show, the first half of a two-part episode, Caine offers to marry a couple. When Caine tells McBurney that he is a priest, McBurney asks for some explanation. Caine starts his explanation by saying of the Shaolin, "We are trained in the martial arts."

McBurney seems pleased. "Marital ceremony," he says, "ought to come easy, then."

Caine says, 'Martial' refers to the arts of war. The word that refers to marriage is 'marital,' a quite similar word for a very different thing."

Episode number:	**38**
Episode title:	**The Cenotaph, Part 2**
Original airdate:	**4-11-74**
Writer:	**William Kelley**
Director:	**Richard Lang**
Guest stars:	**Stefan Gierasch, Michael Pataki,**
	Robert Ridgley, Nancy Kwan,
	Ned Romero, Ed Bakey,
	Ben Cooper, Ivan Naranjo

In the American West, McBurney tells Caine a horrible story: seven years ago, vigilantes paid McBurney to hang a hooded prisoner. The deed done, he discovered he had hanged his beloved Anna.

Caine thinks back to China. Caine tells Mayli, "You are the most beautiful woman I have ever seen, or imagined I would live to see. If what you are is yet not all you are capable of being, I cannot imagine beyond what you are. I cannot imagine but that your soul is quite as beautiful as your body, your face, and that, therefore, I shall learn to love you."

Shortly after, Caine and Mayli make love in a barn. The barn is stormed by Kai Tong. Kai sets fire to the structure and takes off

Mayli Ho (Nancy Kwan) is Caine's love interest in the flashback sequences in "The Cenotaph," Episodes #37 and #38.

with Mayli, leaving Caine for dead in the flames. Nonetheless, Caine survives and comes for Mayli. Kai attacks him with several weapons, all of which Caine effectively dodges.

Back in the West, a posse captures the outlaws who have stolen the gold from the stagecoach. McBurney is forced to open the box in which he had said lay the dead Anna. (McBurney starts to speak of the woman as dead only after she fails to say "I do" when Caine performs a marriage ceremony for him and Anna.) When the box is finally opened, Caine and McBurney discover a granite monolith, carved by wind and weather, into the rough likeness of a woman.

Back in China, Kai gives up, but taunts Caine with his own victory. He tells Caine that Mayli will destroy him. Mayli, realizing Kai has spoken the truth, rejects Caine, though she sobs when he is gone.

In the West, Caine and McBurney bury the monolith. After he eulogizes over the grave, Caine places a memento on the site—one that he has carried all these years. It is a jade pendant given to him by Mayli.

Notes: Part of the reason that so much of this episode (the second part of The Cenotaph) takes place in China, says producer Alex Beaton, is that the production staff was beginning to realize that the American West was invariably the West—that is, predictable. Thus, at the end of this, the second season, there was a turn to Asia. More of the episodes were to be set in China and, in the third season, the show became, decidedly, more mystical.

Caine (David Carradine) communicates with a spiritual crow, in Episode #42, "A Small Beheading."

CHAPTER NINE

Third Season Episodes

Episode number:	**39**
Episode title:	**Cry of the Night Beast**
Original airdate:	**9-21-74**
Writers:	**Abe Polsky, Ed Waters**
Director:	**Richard Lang**
Guest stars:	**Stefanie Powers, Albert Salmi,**
	Don Stroud, Victory Jory, Alex Henteloff,
	Kenneth O'Brien

CAINE RECEIVES an odd, almost supernatural, cry for help that sends him to the side of a young buffalo. He then stops bounty hunter Reuben Branch from killing the animal. Robbed of his prize, Branch promises to get the animal and its mother some other time. The young buffalo, not yet weaned, becomes Caine's special charge.

At the same time, Caine meets Edna, who is expecting a child. Reuben Branch is the father. Caine realizes that Edna is mystically linked with the young buffalo, because one day he hears Edna saying, "Save me, save me." When he looks at her, however, her lips aren't moving. Then, he sees that the sound seems to be coming from the young buffalo's mouth. Odd as it is, Caine understands that Edna will surely die if Branch is successful in killing the young buffalo. "The life force," Caine concludes at the end of the episode, "creates strange attachments."

Notes: Director Richard Lang loved working on the Kung Fu series, though he did have some qualms about this show. He explains: "This hundred-pound baby buffalo was the most difficult performer I encountered during the series. He just did not want to do what the script said. And there were a few tense moments when mommy tried to get to baby and didn't care how or who she went through. Buffaloes don't give a shit about overtime."

Episode number:	**40**
Episode title:	**My Brother, My Executioner**
Original airdate:	**9-28-74**
Writer:	**John T. Dugan**
Director:	**Jerry Thorpe**
Guest stars:	**James Wainwright, Richard Kelton,**
	John Vernon, A Martinez,
	Carol Lawrence, Clay Tanner, Beulah Quo

Caine visits a seer named Mai Chi. She tells him, "I serve only those who pursue illusions." Caine says that is the very reason he has come to her. He, too, may be pursuing an illusion. He is looking for his brother, yet he does not know if he is still alive . . . or, indeed, if he ever lived. Mai Chi tells him, "The man you call brother, the man named Danny Caine, is waiting for you at the end of this journey. But it would be better for him and for you if you would not find him." When he asks why, she says, "Others seek him as you do, and will find him. And Death will be close behind!" Before Caine leaves Mai Chi, she says to him, "Beware, Shaolin! You, too, are not above illusion!"

Soon enough, Caine finds his brother, but the reunion is strange. Danny gives Caine a chilly reception. Caine then learns that a professional gunman, Curley Bill Graham, is looking for his brother, because Danny has a reputation as the West's most skillful gunman. If Curley Bill Graham can defeat Danny, then Graham's reputation as the "Prince of the Pistoleers" will be assured.

Caine intervenes on his brother's behalf and confronts Graham—flesh to firearm. By this time, Caine realizes that he has not truly met his brother, but a Danny-imposter. Caine finally asks the impersonator if Danny is alive. The imposter responds with a long speech:

"We met during the war. Served together. We talked . . . as soldiers do . . . between battles . . . when there's nothing to do but wait. He told me about himself . . . his family. I listened . . . remembered . . . After the war we both wandered . . . in different directions. I was good with this . . . " The imposter indicates his gun. "Too good. But I used it to uphold the law. I never killed anyone except I *had* to. In self-defense. Danny and I would run into each other from time to time. We were always friends . . . even when he was running—from someone . . . or something . . ."

Eventually, the tortured man explains that Danny had given him his past, and the deed to his farm, and the imposter took it because he felt he had to. "Do you understand that?" the imposter says, insistently, to Caine.

Rather than respond, Caine remembers Master Kan's words: "Perhaps the proper conclusion one can come to is not to come easily to conclusions."

Notes: Early on, Caine tells the Danny-imposter, "I was a priest." One wonders why he uses the past tense. It may be that the show's writers caught up to David Carradine's interpretation of the titles that Shaolin graduates were given. Carradine says those who left the temple were "monks" not "priests," although episodes often referred to Caine as a Shaolin priest.

Episode number:	**41**
Episode title:	**The Valley of Terror**
Original airdate:	**10-5-74**
Writers:	**Katharyn and Michael Michaelian**
Director:	**Harry Harris**
Guest stars:	**Sondra Locke, Howard Duff,**
	Jan Sterling, Joe Renteria,
	Ken Swofford, John Quade, James Hong

Caine helps Gwyneth Jenkins after she escapes from a mental institution. Caine realizes she is not mad but that she does have the disarming ability to see into the future. Caine also recognizes the cruel ignorance of those who want to return her to the institution, so he wrests her from their control. In accordance with his training,

Caine then joins Gwyneth, his mysterious charge, in a mystical journey toward "the end of her fear." That journey leads them to a cryptic Indian burial ground. Caine realizes that Gwyneth's mind is an instrument for bringing about good. And, in the end, Gwyneth has a premonition about Caine's search for his lost brother Danny. In her final words to him, she says, "Oh, yes! Yes! He lives! And you'll find him!"

Notes: Caine's mystical journey with Gwyneth is frightening, because it takes him into the hidden parts of his own mind. In a flashback, Caine has an early experience of how disturbing such a journey can be. He meditates very deeply and is terrified by the results.

MASTER KAN: Your heart beats too fast. You must quiet it.

(Young Caine begins the long, slow breathing techniques he has been taught. Master Kan grows more satisfied with his pulse.)

MASTER KAN: What frightened you?
YOUNG CAINE: I heard the Silence, Master.

   Caine describes his experience for Kan, and Kan tells him, "You have experienced Oneness." Caine remarks that the feeling caused him great joy, but at the same time he felt as though he were dying. To help him understand what this feeling is about, Kan asks the boy if he knows the lesson of the silkworm, and the conversation continues as follows:

YOUNG CAINE: The silkworm dies, the moth lives, yet they are not two separate beings, but one and the same.
MASTER KAN: It is the same with a man. His false beliefs must die, so that he may know the joy of the Way. What you felt in the Silence is real. Something in you *is* dying. It is called Ignorance.

Episode number:	**42**
Episode title:	**A Small Beheading**
Original airdate:	**10-12-74**
Writer:	**Eugene Price**
Director:	**Richard Lang**
Guest stars:	**William Shatner, France Nuyen, Rosemary Forsythe, Tony Brubaker, Kinjo Shibuya, James Hong**

Brandywine Gage, a swashbuckling sea captain, tracks down Caine at the ranch where he is working. Gage presents Caine with an official pardon from the emperor (for Caine's killing of the emperor's nephew). Gage reports that he has been commissioned to return Caine to China, so that Caine can submit to the one condition of his pardon: in return for the suspension of the death sentence, Caine must agree to have one of his fingers severed in the presence of the emperor.

Thinking about this unpleasant prospect, Caine remembers when one of his masters tended to a man with an infected finger. The man did not follow the master's instruction, the infection spread, and the arm had to be amputated. All the while, this man feared a black crow that—he was convinced—was a sign of death.

While debating Gage's offer, Caine meets Gage's wife, Lady Ching. She is the late royal nephew's sister. She cannot wait to bring Caine back to China, but she also is the only one Caine believes will tell him the truth about the pardon. When a crow appears, Caine convinces the superstitious Lady Ching that the bird is the spirit of her dead brother. Since Lady Ching believes this, she takes the crow's appearance to be a sign from her dead brother that she should free Caine. Thus, Lady Ching confesses that her husband is lying; there is, in fact, no pardon, and Caine will be killed if he returns to China with Gage.

Caine and Gage come to blows. Caine wins, and Lady Ching, who is satisfied that she has contacted her brother through the black crow, forgives Caine his past transgression.

Notes: Of guest star William Shatner, Radames Pera says, "I was really thrilled to be on the set with him. Of course, this was before the return of *Star Trek* [in which Shatner starred]. So there I was, young Caine—Grasshopper!—meeting Captain Kirk."

In this episode, Caine meets, works for, and falls in love with the rancher Ellie, played by Rosemary Forsythe. In the first season of the show, this might not have happened. Then, Caine was more careful to keep his distance from people in general and women in particular. But as Caine's character developed over the course of the series, he changed.

As Carradine points out, Caine violated certain Shaolin precepts when he began to involve himself in other people's problems. According to what he had been taught in the temple, Caine should have been a mere observer. In the West, he did not fully abandon his teachings; rather, he went beyond them, as he was moved by new circumstances and people.

Episode number:	**43**
Episode title:	**The Predators**
Original airdate:	**10-19-74**
Writers:	**John Menken, Lloyd Richards, Ed Waters**
Director:	**Harry Harris**
Guest stars:	**Cal Bellini, Anthony Zerbe, George DiCenzo,**
	Robert Phillips, Frank Michael Liu

Caine is looking for Rafe, the leader of a gang that makes its living by scalping Apaches for reward money. Caine must find Rafe, because only Rafe can clear him of an attempted murder charge. During his search, Caine befriends a young, vengeful Apache named Hoskay, whom he saves from Rafe's band. Eventually, Hoskay and Caine meet up with Rafe, who doesn't want to come with Caine. Caine then has a hand-to-hand encounter with a Navajo member of the scalpers so he can mask his own plan to kidnap Rafe. At the conclusion of the fight, Caine knocks Rafe off a high cliff and jumps after him. Then, Caine, Rafe, and Hoskay make their way out of a wilderness canyon as they are stalked by the angry Navajo and the rest of the scalper gang.

In the end, Rafe clears Caine's name, and in the process, loses his "job" as head of the gang. Caine asks him if he regrets his loss, and Rafe says sardonically, "Nothing else is gonna pay as good."

Notes: In addition to missing the money, Rafe admits, too, that he liked to kill because it gave him "a special feeling." Rafe doesn't seem to see Apaches as humans. Not surprisingly, earlier, Caine felt compelled to say to Rafe, "I am not a Chinaman, not a breed. I am a man whose name is Kwai Chang Caine."

Episode number:	**44**
Episode title:	**The Vanishing Image**
Original airdate:	**11-1-74**
Writer:	**Gustave Field**
Director:	**Barry Crane**
Guest stars:	**Lew Ayres, Tom Nardini, Benson Fong,**
	Jonathan Hole, Bill Saito

Caine searches for Beaumont, a photographer who, he hopes, can identify a picture that *might* be of Caine's brother Danny. Once he finds Beaumont, Caine realizes Beaumont is dying, because he has been inhaling mercury fumes over the course of many years of developing photos.

Flashing back to his youth in China, Caine recalls Li Yu, a beggar who collected broken bits of porcelain to sculpt his life's work. The young Caine had thought Li Yu foolish.

YOUNG CAINE: He prizes what is worthless.
MASTER PO: To you . . . to me, perhaps. Not worthless to him.
YOUNG CAINE: Bits and pieces that cannot be put back together . . . ?
MASTER PO: Not to understand a man's purpose does not make *him* confused.

Back in the Old West, Matsoka, a teenage Indian boy vows to kill Beaumont for stealing his Spirit by taking his picture. Caine means to protect Beaumont, but he is delayed in his efforts to get to the photographer's cabin, because Sai Si, a member of the Order of the Avenging Dragon, follows Caine and challenges him to a ritual combat to avenge Caine's killing of the emperor's nephew. Caine agrees to fight, but asks Sai Si if the combat can wait. "Sai Si," Caine explains, "it is possible a needless death may occur. You must allow me to prevent it." Sai Si, refusing to wait, throws one of his swords toward Caine. Reluctantly, Caine picks up the weapon, and the two men fight—sword to sword, then sword against no sword when Caine's weapon is damaged, and finally hand-to-hand. The fight is distinguished by the dramatic leaps the men take as they move about the craggy terrain, sometimes jumping off of boulders, sometimes fighting in the river. Eventually, Caine prevails over his artful opponent. He runs to Beaumont's cabin, reaching the photographer

The itinerant photographer Beaumont (Lew Ayres) gives Caine information about his half-brother Danny, in Episode #44, "The Vanishing Image."

in time to protect him from the angry Matsoka, but not from the illness to which Beaumont eventually succumbs.

Notes: In a flashback, the sculptor Li Yu also dies. Master Po tells the tearful Caine that "death has had no victory." Confused, Caine says, "But Li Yu is gone. . . ."

Master Po gestures to the incomplete yet noble structure that Li Yu was working on at the time of his death and says, "Is he not still here . . . in this work of beauty that was his life?"

Episode number:	45
Episode title:	**Blood of the Dragon, Part 1**
Original airdate:	**11-8-74**
Writer:	**John T. Dugan**
Director:	**Richard Lang**
Guest stars:	**Eddie Albert, Patricia Neal, Season Hubley, Clyde Kusatsu**

Caine arrives in the town of Gurneyville, where he soundlessly walks down Main Street to the barbershop. The sheriff is being shaved by Vinnie, the barber. Vinnie is also the town coroner/undertaker/embalmer. Caine's manner is somewhat mysterious as he politely asks to see the body of the man who died in town the previous night. At first, the sheriff hesitates, but then he grants Caine his wish. When the sheriff lifts the sheet off the body, Caine says, "His name is Henry Rafael Caine . . . my grandfather."

As the body is prepared for burial, Caine is approached by Dr. George Baxter, who knew Henry. Caine tells Baxter that he found a bullet hole in his grandfather's body. Unsettled by this news, Baxter rides out to the Kingsley Ranch, where he is greeted by twins Johnny and Margit McLean. It turns out their grandmother, Sara Kingsley, was part of a love triangle that involved Baxter and Henry Caine. For years, Sara has kept the secret that her daughter—Margit and Johnny's mother—was the illegitimate child of Henry Caine. Sara Kingsley transfers her anger about that birth from Henry Caine to Kwai Chang Caine.

Notes: As with other episodes, this one is complicated by the fact that men from China are looking for Caine and the fact that the "Wanted"

Dr. George Baxter (Eddie Albert) and Caine consider the mystery of Caine's grandfather's murder, in Episode #45, "Blood of the Dragon, Part 1."

poster, bearing Caine's name, is seen by people in town. The unresolved tension at the end carries the story—and viewers—ahead to the next show, the second part of "Blood of the Dragon."

Episode number:	**46**
Episode title:	**Blood of the Dragon, Part 2**
Original airdate:	**11-15-74**
Writer:	**John T. Dugan**
Director:	**Richard Lang**
Guest stars:	**Eddie Albert, Edward Albert,**
	Patricia Neal, Season Hubley, Clyde Kusatsu

Conversation between Johnny McLean and Sara Kingsley reveals that Johnny murdered Henry Rafael Caine at his grandmother's urging. Kwai Chang Caine approaches Sara Kingsley with this realization. Sara barely responds to the accusation, but then she asks him what he is going to do about it. Caine does not have an answer for her.

Meanwhile, Margit sees a "Wanted" poster for Caine. Hoping to protect her brother, she telegrams information about Caine's whereabouts to China. Later, she realizes Caine's true nature and apologizes for what she has done, but it is too late. Three extremely talented fighters from the Order of the Avenging Dragon in China arrive and challenge Caine to combat to avenge the death of the emperor's nephew. Caine prepares to meet these deadly adversaries, when Johnny comes galloping toward him on a horse. Johnny draws his gun, but before he shoots, Caine talks calmly with him and reveals their common bond. Johnny is horrified to learn that he has killed his own grandfather.

Caine is forced to fight himself when a demon Kwai Chang Caine is conjured up by the Order of the Avenging Dragon, in Epsiode #46, "Blood of the Dragon, Part 2."

Subsequently, Caine fights his Chinese adversaries. Johnny comes to defend him and is killed in the fight. After Johnny is buried, Caine must go back to a pavilion to fight those of the Triad who remain. Caine enters the pavilion. In the pavilion are Margit and one of the members of the Triad—Han Su Lok, who is shaking. Margit seems to be in a sort of trance. Suddenly, a life-size demon appears. Caine knows this demon. It is the essence of evil—the *demon* Kwai Chang Caine, the demon who lives in the dark corners of every person's mind. Then, Sara Kingsley enters. Right after that, a life-size demon of Sara enters the tent and engulfs her.

Caine fights as he has never fought before and finally, through his power of concentration, defeats Han Su Lok and the demon. After the fight, Margit and Caine find the lifeless body of Sara on the beach.

Notes: In a flashback, young Caine wonders if evil demons exist. Master Kan responds by saying, "Do wars, famine, disease and death exist? Do lust, greed and hate exist? . . . They are man's creations . . . brought into being by the dark side of his nature."

Episode number:	**47**
Episode title:	**The Demon God**
Original airdate:	**11-22-74**
Writers:	**George Clayton Johnson, David Michael Korn**
Director:	**David Carradine**
Guest stars:	**Brian Tochi, Victor-Sen Yung, Michael Greene, Robert Tessier, Brenda Venus, Tad Horino**

The young Caine is in China with a prince named Shen Ung. In an attempt to "see" what death is, Shen Ung poisons the young Caine. Shen Ung wants to question Caine as he dies, so he can relay the information about what he sees to his own dying father.

In a state of delirium, Caine is catapulted into the future, where the adult Caine is also facing death, because he has been stung by a scorpion and has fallen into a mountain cave opening, where he will soon be buried by an avalanche.

While young Caine is forced to discuss life and death with Shen Ung, the adult Caine is confronted, in his delirium, by a ghostly Aztec priest, a warrior, and a seductive woman. The priest, warrior, and woman offer the adult Caine life and pleasure if he will only accept their strange god, Attyl.

In the end, young Caine outwits the prince, and Master Kan comes to the rescue with an antidote to the poison. The adult Caine stands firm in his own beliefs and rejects the evil before him. In the episode's climax, both Caines—young and mature—receive the reward of life, and the present merges with the past.

Notes: This is the first episode of the show that David Carradine directed. After the script was purchased, the producers didn't quite know what to do with it. "They were," Carradine says, "afraid of it. I said, 'I want to direct one.' And they said, 'Great, give him this one.' And I think there may have been some people who said, 'Okay, give him this one and watch him fall on his face. . . . And I think there were other people who said, 'Maybe he can find a way out of it.'"

This episode starts with a flashback and then uses the device of a flash-*forward*. Carradine liked the script because it put Radames Pera at the center of a show. It also was one of the few episodes in which Master Kan got to display his physical skills. Kan knocks a couple of guards to the side when he comes to rescue Caine. Then he carries Caine to the apothecary. The scene shows sides of Kan rarely displayed—his compassion and his strength. "Suddenly," David Carradine says of the character of Master Kan, "you see why he is a master . . . instead of them just talking about it all the time."

In this episode, Caine, while wounded, recalls the words of Lao-tzu: "He who is open eyed is open minded. He who is open minded is open hearted. He who is open hearted is kingly. He who is kingly is Godly. He who is Godly is useful. He who is useful is infinite. He who is infinite is immune. He who is immune is immortal."

Episode number:	**48**
Episode title:	**The Devil's Champion**
Original airdate:	**12-20-74**
Writers:	**Katharyn and Michael Michaelian, David Michael Korn**
Director:	**Robert Lewis**
Guest stars:	**Richard Loo, Soon-Teck Oh, Frank Michael Liu, Victoria Racimo, John Fujioka**

In China Yi Lien challenges Master Kan to a ritualistic combat to the death. He gives no reason for his challenge. Kan has no knowledge of the man, so, at first, he refuses to accept the challenge. Then Yi Lien threatens to kill an innocent peasant for every day his challenge goes unanswered. Kan has no choice but to respond. It is decided, however, that before Yi Lien can be deemed worthy of fighting Master Kan, he must fight the young disciple Huo in a preliminary battle.

Meanwhile, Caine has an odd vision regarding the mysterious warrior, but he is unable to interpret it. Also, Lady Mei, Yi Lien's sister, shows up. She, too, cannot explain her brother's strange behavior, and she is frightened for his life.

Caine's vision reappears and reveals the source of Yi Lien's power—and his evil desire. Yi Lien is possessed by the devil Hsiang. Caine journeys to Hsiang's lair and defeats him—saving Yi Lien and his colleague Huo in the process.

Notes: In the climactic scene of this episode set completely in China, Caine fights Hsiang, while Yi and Huo fight. If Caine can defeat Hsiang, he

Caine battles the evil Hsiang (John Fujioka) in Episode #48, "The Devil's Champion"

can also save Huo, for Yi has been given supernatural powers by Hsiang. Caine's efforts are hampered by the fact that Hsiang doubles, then quadruples his own image, so Caine is surrounded by illusions, as well as his real foe. Then Lady Mei appears in the midst of the fight—but it is unclear if it is the real Lady Mei or Hsiang in disguise. Eventually, however, Caine prevails, and Hsiang is disappointed in his desire to ruin the Shaolin temple by killing Kan and then encouraging masters and disciples to turn on one another.

Episode number:	**49**
Episode title:	**The Garments of Rage**
Original airdate:	**1-11-75**
Writers:	**Theodore Apstein, Ed Waters, Herman Miller**
Director:	**Marc Daniels**
Guest stars:	**James Shigeta, James Olson, James Hong, Harrison Page**

In the Old West, a railroad sustains a series of attacks by a mysterious assailant whom no one has ever seen or heard. A young boy catches a glimpse of this phantom, but his identity is otherwise unknown. When Caine shows up looking for work, he is interrogated by an investigator named Damion, but the young boy says Caine is not the guilty party.

Soon, Caine—who has been drawn to the railroad site telepathically—is confronted by one of his former teachers, Master Li, who has come to live in America. Caine learns that Li's nephew was accidentally killed by a train, and Li is now seeking revenge.

Meanwhile, investigator Damion, sensing Caine knows more than he is willing to admit, tries to enlist his help. Caine declines but knows he must confront his former teacher. Before he has a chance to do this, Li lures Damion into the forest and prepares to kill him, but Caine intervenes and saves the investigator.

Notes: Once safe, Damion decides he has done his last job for the railroad. Then, Damion and Caine have the following conversation:

DAMION: I'm leaving too. I don't have to help them devour men. There's other things I can do to earn my keep.
CAINE: You will not improve anything by going away.
DAMION: But I don't have to be a part of it. I think that's something I picked up from you.
CAINE: Did I say that?
DAMION: You don't have to put everything in words. I catch on.

Episode number:	50
Episode title:	**Besieged, Part 1: Death on Cold Mountain**
Original airdate:	**1-18-75**
Writers:	**William Kelley, Ed Waters, David Michael Korn**
Director:	**David Carradine**
Guest stars:	**Barbara Seagull (Hershey), Victor-Sen Yung,**
	Khigh Dheigh, Richard Narita, Brian Fong, Yuki Shimoda

In China, the fierce warlord Sing Lu Chan demands that Nan Chi marry him. She refuses. For revenge, Sing Lu Chan destroys the Shaolin temple at Fukien where Nan Chi is staying. The survivors of the attack hide in the cave of an old man named Tamo. Tamo then goes to Honan and asks Master Kan if the survivors may come to Honan. Kan says yes and sends Master Po and Caine to bring the survivors to Honan.

The three travel to the cave safely, but on the way back to the Shaolin temple in Honan, Sing attacks them. Po and Tamo are taken captive. Caine delivers the others to the temple in Honan and then returns to help his captured friends. Caine is able to rescue Po and Tamo, but Sing is in close pursuit.

In effort to distract Sing, Tamo drives a cart pell-mell towards a steep cliff. He topples over, apparently falling to his death. Po and Caine have no choice but to continue on without Tamo.

Eventually the two make it safely back to Honan, where Nan Chi challenges Caine to an encounter to prove her right to become a Shaolin. Before Caine can consider the challenge, Sing arrives and threatens to destroy the Honan temple—if Nan Chi refuses to surrender.

Notes: Of the late Victor-Sen Yung, who plays Tamo in this episode, Carradine tells this true story: "Sen Yung was on an airplane which was commandeered by a terrorist. And he took the gun away from the terrorist and was wounded in the process. He was actually a real hero. . . . And he was probably the best actor that we had on the show."

Early on in the episode, when Po goes to help Tamo, Kan reveals Po's age. Po is eighty-three. At another point, Kan welcomes Nan Chi and others to the temple and introduces himself as Chen Ming Kan. (This is the first time we learn Kan's full name.)

Later in the episode, Tamo and Po tell Caine, Nan Chi, and a third young student to proceed to the safety of the Shaolin temple in Honan while Tamo and Po stay behind to fight the pursuers. Caine refuses to go. He does not want to leave his master in danger. Po says, "Grasshopper. . . . Tamo's plan is best for all of us. I know your affection for me, but in this case it is misguided."

Still later in this episode, we see sides of Kan we have not previously seen. With her gender disguised, Nan Chi says to Master Kan, "I might wish to be Shaolin, Master—But I would not be acceptable as a monk."

Kan responds, "Perhaps you had better let me be the judge of that." Nan Chi lifts her hood. Kan is clearly surprised. He says, "Well, I am sorry that we are not so advanced."

Angry that Kan will not even consider her, even though she has (while disguised as a boy) already proven her skill, Nan Chi says, "You cannot refuse me."

A bit disconcerted, Master Kan says, "I am Master of Monks, here." He explains that the Honan temple has neither the facility nor the desire to

Nan Chi (Barbara Seagull/Hershey) and Caine flee for safety, in Episode #50, "Besieged, Part 1."

house nuns. Nan Chi says that now he has the opportunity to change that. Kan responds with a rare scolding: "I do not regard it as an opportunity, and I certainly do not regard you as a remedy. I regard you, on the contrary, as a remarkably impudent child whose unacceptability is only exceeded by her capacity for showing disrespect."

Nan Chi responds, "Surely not because I am a woman. . . ."

There is a pause and Kan acknowledges the girl's right to a trial of the issue by combat. Between Nan Chi's line and Kan's acknowledgment, the script for this episode reads: "Master Kan is most cruelly caught out . . . not because of dishonesty or duplicity . . . but simply because of a centuries-laden way of thinking of females. Hell yes, it's because she's a woman . . . and the truth of it hangs in the echoes . . . and Master Kan is too honest an old man to deny the truth."

Episode number:	**51**
Episode title:	**Besieged, Part 2: Cannon at the Gates**
Original airdate:	**1-25-75**
Writers:	**William Kelley, Ed Waters, David Michael Korn**
Director:	**David Carradine**
Guest stars:	**Barbara Seagull (Hershey), Victor-Sen Yung, Khigh Dheigh, Richard Narita, Brian Fong, Yuki Shimoda**

Master Kan rations the temple's food supply and establishes a watch on Sing's troops. Caine continues to spend time with Nan Chi. Sing finally sends his captain—Shun Low—to capture the monks. Nan Chi decides she should surrender to Sing, but Shun Low stops her and takes her into custody. It turns out he is a traitor to Sing, but that does not mean he is a friend to Nan Chi. In fact, Shun Low wants to overthrow Sing, destroy the temple, and establish himself as a new warlord. Caine saves Nan Chi. In the process, he is knocked unconscious, and Shun Low tries to kill him. To protect him, Nan Chi throws herself in front of Caine and sustains a fatal blow. Tamo, who everyone thought had died, shows up and is ready to defend the Honan temple. Sing, however, no longer has a motive for sacking the temple since Nan Chi is dead. He stops the impending battle, and the monks are left to pay their respects to Nan Chi.

Notes: Carradine reports that he shaved his head so that he could both direct and act in this two-part story. Without a shaved head, he would have had to spend three to four hours in makeup every day. This might have left him enough time to star in "Besieged," but not also to direct.

Episode number:	52
Episode title:	**A Lamb to the Slaughter**
Original airdate:	**2-8-75**
Writers:	**Robert Specht, David Michael Korn**
Director:	**Harry Harris**
Guest stars:	**Alejandro Rey, Barbara Luna,**
	Joe Santos, Julio Medina,
	Roberto Contreras, Richard Yniguez,
	Stephen Manley

Caine goes to a Mexican village in order to repay a debt. Years ago, a man lost his life in the process of saving Caine's father's life. Now, Caine finds the son of this man. The son, named Matteo, refuses Caine's gesture, for he feels that one cannot repay such a debt; besides, he feels that his mother's life was ruined by his father's death.

Caine steps aside and waits for another opportunity to honor his obligation. The chance arrives when Caine realizes Matteo's village is under the imposed protection of a gang leader named Sanjero. When Matteo's teenage brother dies in his attempt to shoot Sanjero, Matteo tells Caine that there is a way for the debt to be repaid after all. Then, he asks Caine to teach him to kill. Caine is reluctant but remembers Master Po taught him that a debt of honor must be repaid in the manner requested. Caine's instructions improve Matteo's fighting skills, and when Matteo next battles Sanjero, he wins. However, Caine is able to stop him from killing his opponent.

Notes: In a practice fight, Matteo ineffectively attacks Caine with a sharpened stick. Frustrated, Matteo rushes at Caine and grabs Caine in a bear hug. Caine does not resist Matteo. Instead, he allows himself to be lifted from the ground. Then, Caine winces and starts to struggle. He says to Matteo, "You are . . . strong." Matteo arrogantly asks Caine if he thought he was weak. Caine says, "No. . . . Not weak," then he balls his own hands into fists, extends his thumbs, and, without any great force, jabs his thumbs at the side of Matteo's thick neck. Matteo's arms drop to his sides, and he says, "You did something. I can't feel my arms. What'd you do?" Seconds later, Matteo is able to move his arms, but he remains bewildered.

Caine explains, "The body is the arrow, the spirit is the bow. You must learn to use the strength of the spirit."

Episode number:	**53**
Episode title:	**One Step into Darkness**
Original airdate:	**2-15-75**
Writer:	**Gerald Sanford**
Teleplay:	**Theodore Apstein, Robert Sherman**
Director:	**Marc Daniels**
Guest stars:	**Leslie Ann Charleson, David Huddleston, Bruce Carradine, Byron Mabe, Stephen Manley, Frances Fong, A. Wilford Brimley**

Captain Roy Starbuck has been having a difficult time with his wife, Amy, who has been acting peculiarly recently. Caine feels a mysterious link to Amy, but he does not know why. Soon, Caine learns that Amy has a drug addiction that is being fed by a local businessman and that she is deeply saddened by her loss, years ago, of a baby in childbirth. When Caine comes to her rescue, her husband thinks Caine is his wife's lover, and he has Caine arrested. Eventually, Caine convinces Captain Starbuck otherwise. Then, Caine recalls how Master Po told him to seek out his own demon in order to be rid of it.

Not long after, Caine finds himself on a mystical journey into Amy's metaphysical world. Once in this realm, he asks Amy, "What do you call this place?"

She answers, "Heaven . . . It *is* like heaven, isn't it?"

She explains that she goes to this place whenever she is lost or in doubt. Suddenly, her manner changes, and a demon starts to speak through her mouth. The demon says that he made a pact with Caine long ago. In a flashback, we see the boy Caine, delirious with fever. We see through his blurred and distorted eyes. A doctor and nurse are above him, a young girl is dying in the bed next to him. We hear a doctors voice say that the girl, like the boy, needs a miracle to survive. Speaking to a figure on a water pitcher next to his bed, the boy Caine says, "If you must take one, take her. Please . . . take her. Let me live. . . ."

Back in the present, the demon starts to impersonate the voice of Master Po. Then, the demon mimics Amy's voice. Finally, he shifts into his own voice and says, "You are alive only because you asked me to take the life of a little girl!" Caine does not accept this judgment, however; he knows that the demon is not real, but the embodiment of his worst fears. Caine tells the demon, "Long before I created you, it was written that she would die and I would live. The wish of a frightened boy does not change the ways of Destiny." The demon commands Caine to die. Caine commands the demon to disappear, to become nothing. There is no physical fight, but Caine wins the spiritual struggle, and the Demon slowly fades away, as Caine returns to the "real" world.

Notes: David Carradine's brother Bruce played Captain Starbuck in this episode. David Huddleston, who also appeared in Episode #22, played the local businessman feeding Amy's drug habit. Huddleston went on to play the character of Kevin's grandfather in the TV series *The Wonder Years*. A. Wilford Brimley, who had a bit role in this episode, went on to star in the *Cocoon* movies of the late 1980s.

Episode number:	**54**
Episode title:	**The Thief of Chendo**
Original airdate:	**2-22-75**
Writers:	**Bernard B. Bossick, Lary H. Gibson, Simon Muntner, Norman Katkov**
Director:	**Harry Harris**
Guest stars:	**Harushi, James Hong, Claire Nono, John Fujioka, Beulah Quo,**

**Jeanne Joe, Bill Saito,
Tad Horino**

Tien, a beloved ruler and Chinese grand duke, sends his ring to
Master Po as a signal that he needs help. Caine is dispatched to
Tien's aid, just as the ring gives off a strange signal that portends
danger for Tien's royal city of Chendo.

In the city, Caine learns that Tien is dead and Chun Yen, the
new grand duke, has begun a reign of terror in Chendo. Caine also
meets up with Sing Tao, a thief, last of the Sainted and Honorable
Guild of Thieves. Sing Tao complains that the order is dying out,
that it was once easy to be a "respectable" thief, but it is now
impossible, for Chun Yen takes everything in the city for himself.

Later, Chun Yen mistakes Caine and Sing Tao for priests and
takes the two young men prisoner. He tells them that they must
perform a marriage ceremony that he has arranged for Tien's daughter against her will. Caine and Sing Tao steal away and discover
that Tien is not dead but imprisoned in Chun Yen's palace. Together,
Caine and Sing Tao manage to depose the evil Chun Yen and
restore Tien to power.

*Caine befriends
Jonno Marcado
(Jose Feliciano), a
blind musician,
in Episode #55,
"Battle Hymn."*

Notes: Early on, Caine asks Sing
Tao, "In what temple does one
learn the art of thievery?" Later,
after Caine suggests that Sing Tao
give up his thieving ways, Sing Tao
is aghast.

SING TAO: You ask me to give
up my life's *work*?
CAINE: In an emergency one
must take emergency measures.
SING TAO: Would you give up
your priesthood?
CAINE: I am not dissatisfied
with my lot.

Episode number:	**55**
Episode title:	**Battle Hymn**
Original airdate:	**3-1-75**
Writer:	**Dorothy C. Fontanna**
Director:	**Barry Crane**
Guest stars:	**Jose Feliciano, Julian Adderley, Beverly Garland, Joe Maross**

In the American Southwest, Caine plans to take the remains of a bounty hunter to the dead man's family in Sovalo, a small town thirty miles away. On his way, Caine meets a pair of traveling musicians—the blind Jonno Marcada, and Trim Delavalle—who are heading to Sovalo, too. Jonno spent his boyhood in Sovalo, and he had an early transcendental experience there that he wants to repeat.

In Sovalo, they find Mrs. Hobart, the bounty hunter's widow. She and the local lawman, Sheriff Barrow, seem less concerned about Hobart's death than about a map that they know is hidden in the dead man's belongings. The map is the key to a rich silver deposit, and both the widow and the sheriff are ready to kill for it. While searching for the map, the sheriff imprisons Caine, Jonno, and Trim. The imprisonment triggers a lynch mob who suspect the trio of having murdered the bounty hunter. The trio escape when Caine defeats the entire mob single-handedly with kung-fu. Then, they set out to find the place that Jonno vaguely remembers from his youth, the site of his previous transcendental experience. The spot ends up being a cave, illuminated—at select moments— by a beautiful, single sparkling shaft of light. Just as Jonno and his friends arrive in the cave, the sheriff and Mrs. Hobart appear, for they have discovered that the cave is the source of the silver. Technically, Jonno, as the eldest of the town's Marcada clan, has title to the mine. Should he die, the title will pass to his cousin Raoul, who is easy to manipulate. Knowing all this, three "heavies" also show up at the mine in the hopes that they can bury Jonno, Caine, and Trim in the cave and force Raoul into giving them the title. In the end, there is a showdown between all these competing interests. Caine dispatches the heavies while Mrs. Hobart kills Barrow and then is buried by a cave-in that she begins.

Despite all this death, Jonno, Caine, and Trim do experience the mystical moment that they sought. They leave the cave spiritually renewed, ready to continue on their separate paths.

Notes: In this episode, Po and Caine have the following conversation:

YOUNG CAINE: Sometimes, Master, it seems a wall lies between myself and others—a wall through which I may see, but may not touch.

MASTER PO: You feel the fault within yourself.

YOUNG CAINE: I do not know where the fault lies. But I feel . . . apart.

MASTER PO: In your conversation with this other, more is left unsaid than is said.

YOUNG CAINE: It is so.

MASTER PO: Who can know himself well enough to speak all? Who is so well founded to hear all? The sage says: 'Shape clay into a vessel; cut doors and windows for a room; it is the spaces within which make it useful.' So we must listen for the spaces between us.

World-famous guitarist Jose Feliciano played the role of Jonno in this episode, and jazz alto saxophonist Julian Adderley that of Trim. The show was Adderley's first and Feliciano's second dramatic TV role. The title of the episode comes from the rendition of the "The Battle Hymn of the Republic" that the two traveling musicians sing.

Episode number:	56
Episode title:	**The Forbidden Kingdom**
Original airdate:	**3-8-75**
Writers:	**Bernard B. Bossick, Lary H. Gibson**
Director:	**Gordon Hessler**
Guest stars:	**James Shigeta, Adele Yoshioka,**
	Clyde Kusatsu, Evan Kim, Bob Okazaki

In the months immediately after he killed the royal emperor's nephew, Caine flees from the emperor's soldiers in general and from Colonel Lin Pei in particular. Caine goes to a village to seek the assistance of Sou Kin, who has a document that will facilitate Caine's safe passage out of China. On the way to Sou Kin, Caine must trust a villager named Po Li to help him. She is a lovely woman, and she says she will help, but her brother is being held captive by Colonel Lin Pei. Her real plan is to exchange Caine's life for that of her brother. The colonel agrees to this plan—though he has no intention of honoring his word. Still, Po Li believes him, and she guides Caine to Sou Kin. Caine is able to escape the trap she has set. He eludes the soldiers and escapes China.

Episode number:	57
Episode title:	**The Last Raid**
Original airdate:	**3-15-75**
Writer:	**John T. Dugan**
Director:	**Alex Beaton**
Guest stars:	**Hal Williams, L. Q. Jones,**
	Charles Aidman, Charles Haid,
	Hoke Howell, Mae Mercer

Out west, Caine comes back into the lives of ex-slave Caleb Brown and his son Daniel—both of whom he met a year earlier. Now, Caine ministers to the needs of the Brown family and another family, as both Daniel and the other family's son, Jimmy, are kidnapped by members of a remnant Confederate band. After much conflict, Caine finds the boys and saves them. In the end, Daniel tells his father and Jimmy, "You know what Caine says? According to the Chinese Code, whenever someone saves another's life, he's responsible for him . . . *forever.*"

Jimmy responds, "Then . . . I'spose we're *all* gonna be responsible for each other from here on out!"

Notes: The Brown family originally appeared in "The Well" (Episode #16), the first show of the second *Kung Fu* season.

Episode number:	58
Episode title:	**Ambush**
Original airdate:	**3-22-75**
Writer:	**Norman Katkov**
Director:	**Gordon Hessler**
Guest stars:	**John Carradine, Rhonda Fleming, Pat Morita,**
	Timothy Carey, Kay E. Kuter, Bill Mims

Serenity Johnson, Caine's blind old friend, shows up. He plays on Caine's sympathies to force the Shaolin to "be his eyes" as he sets out for Arizona City to claim back a two-thousand-dollar debt. Serenity wants to save his church with the money. The person who owes the money is Jennie Malone, a beautiful saloonkeeper. On their arrival, Jennie agrees to repay her debt if Serenity will help her outfox the most dangerous man in Arizona by taking her secret treasure safely to San Francisco. Caine and Serenity agree to help Jennie in this undertaking. They encounter and overcome many dangers along the way.

Notes: This episode was one of the rare ones in which there were no visual flashbacks—only audio flashbacks, as when Caine recalls this conversation:

CAINE: People in need will call on me for help.
MASTER PO: And will you help them?
CAINE: With all my heart.
MASTER PO: Though there will be difficulty and danger for you.
CAINE: Yes, Master.

Also, this episode marks the third and final appearance of Serenity Johnson, the recurring character played previously by David Carradine's father, John, in episodes #2 and #36.

Episode number:	59
Episode title:	**Barbary House**
Original airdate:	**3-29-75**
Writers:	**Stephen and Elinor Karpf**
Director:	**Marc Daniels**
Guest stars:	**Leslie Nielsen, Lois Nettleton, Tim McIntire, John Lupton, John Blyth Barrymore, Ted Gehring**

Caine's search for his half-brother takes him to the Barbary House, a palace of delights that caters to the appetites of the jaded rich, in San Francisco. Caine soon discovers that gangster Vincent Corbino, owner of the establishment, is blackmailing Danny by holding Zeke, Danny's son, at the Barbary House. Apparently, Danny and Corbino had a business dispute and Corbino will not rest till he finds and destroys Danny. Caine also learns that Delonia Cartell, a rich socialite, is Zeke's mother. Corbino uses Caine's attachment to Zeke to force Caine into becoming a prize fighter at the Barbary House. After a series of fights, Caine takes Delonia and Zeke away from Corbino. Then he sets off to find Danny before Corbino does.

Notes: This is the first of a four-part story line that ended the original series. Leslie Nielsen played Vincent Corbino in this and the subsequent episodes. A talented dramatic actor, Nielsen's recent work has drawn on his abundant comedic talents. After starring in the short-lived TV series *Police Squad* in 1982, Nielsen went on to make the popular Naked Gun theatrical films.

Episode number:	**60**
Episode title:	**Flight to Orion**
Original airdate:	**4-5-75**
Writers:	**Stephen and Elinor Karpf**
Director:	**Marc Daniels**
Guest stars:	**Lois Nettleton, Leslie Nielsen,**
	John Blyth Barrymore, John Lupton,
	Vad de Vargas, Don Keefer,
	Ned Romero, Ted Gehring

Caine guides Delonia and Zeke through a desert wilderness, beset by Indians. A two-hundred-man search party follows; they are determined to kill Caine before he reaches Danny. Then, they intend to kill Danny to earn the $10,000 reward posted by Danny's implacable enemy, Vincent Corbino.

As they flee from Corbino and his men, Delonia is bitten by a rattlesnake. She dies and then Zeke is captured by Corbino when Caine is distracted by a battle with hostile Indians. In the end, Caine appears and chases Corbino away.

Notes: Writer Elinor Karpf reports that Corbino was "the gambling-godfather type," transported to a western setting. This type of enemy, she notes, would reappear in many later martial arts films.

Episode number:	**61**
Episode title:	**The Brothers Caine**
Original airdate:	**4-12-75**
Writers:	**Stephen and Elinor Karpf**
Director:	**Harry Harris**

Guest stars:	Leslie Nielsen, Tim McIntire,
	John Vernon, Joanna Moore,
	John Blyth Barrymore, Carl Weathers,
	Frank Michael Liu

Caine and his nephew Zeke—with Vincent Corbino and his men hot on their trail—look for Danny's hideout in the small town of Orion. Only the widow Lula Morgan knows where the hiding place is. She agrees to sell this information to the highest bidder. In order to secure enough money to save his father, Zeke decides to sell himself to his rich grandfather, General Cantrell, who wants to keep Zeke to himself because the boy is his last remaining relative. Corbino responds to Zeke's move by employing a sinister man, Bad Sam, to arrange for Danny to kill Kwai Chang Caine unknowingly.

Notes: When half-brothers Danny and Kwai Chang Caine finally meet in these final episodes, Kwai Chang Caine responds to the meeting with his usual reserve. Still, it is clear how much Danny means to Kwai Chang—more, at first, than Kwai Chang means to Danny, since Danny is absorbed with saving his own life. Later, Danny will develop a grudging respect and, finally, love for his brother.

Originally, says Elinor Karpf, the writers had thought to complicate the portrait of Danny Caine by having him be a man constantly haunted with nightmares of Chinese men pursuing him. The bad dreams were to have been Danny's version of the Anglo prejudice that he inherited from his family, the family that was so horrified by the union (between their American son and a Chinese woman) that produced Kwai Chang Caine.

In the end, most of the issues of Anglo prejudice were played out by General Cantrell and emerged in the final episode of the series when it is revealed that General Cantrell had a relationship with a Mexican woman.

Episode number:	62
Episode title:	**Full Circle**
Original airdate:	**4-19-75**
Writers:	**Stephen and Elinor Karpf**
Director:	**Marc Daniels**
Guest stars:	**Leslie Nielsen, John Vernon,**
	Tim McIntire, John Blyth Barrymore,
	Ted Gehring, A Martinez,
	Jacques Aubuchon

While brothers Kwai Chang and Danny Caine go off to fight Corbino and his men, Danny's son Zeke honors his word and goes off to live with Cantrell—even though what he really wants is to be with his father. Cantrell is determined to keep Zeke for himself because he takes Zeke to be his last remaining relative, and he wants the family fortune to pass to him. In fact, Tigre, Cantrell's Mexican foreman is also Cantrell's son. Finally, Cantrell is forced to recognize this hidden aspect of his past.

Meanwhile, Corbino, knowing Danny will come looking for Zeke, sets a trap in Cantrell's home. This leads to a fatal show-down—with Danny, Caine, Zeke, Cantrell, and Tigre entangled in the dramatic conclusion. Corbino is defeated. Caine, Danny, and Zeke are brought together.

Kwai Chang Caine is happy his journey is completed, but he feels he must move on.

Notes: Caine literally "bows out" of the episode—that is, he bows, the screen fades to black, and the original *Kung Fu* series comes to an end. One wonders, perhaps, why Caine doesn't stay with his brother. David Carradine offers a possible explanation when he says, "The basic principle of the Taoist teachings is that goals don't matter. You climb the mountain and you never get to the top of it. If you got to the top of it, what are you going to do then? You can sit on it, I suppose, and drink tea and meditate. Or you have to walk down the other side and walk back into a city."

At first Chung Wang (Brandon Lee, at left) and his father, Kwai Chang Caine (David Carradine), do not see eye-to-eye in Kung Fu: The Movie *(1986).*

CHAPTER TEN

The Return of Caine

DAVID CARRADINE credits himself with "shutting down" the *Kung Fu* series in 1975. He explains that he never wanted the series to run for more than three years. He was so adamant about this that he never had a contract during the run of the original series (the contracts he was asked to sign always insisted on a five-year commitment).

The "return" of *Kung Fu* is also, in part, Carradine's doing. In the 1980s, the "return" was marked by one made-for-TV movie and a summer pilot, and a cameo by Carradine as Caine in 1988 in *Gambler Four: The Luck of the Draw* (a TV movie with Kenny Rogers in which several classic western heroes made a brief appearance). In the 1990s, the "return" is marked by a new series, in which Carradine once again plays the lead role.

Originally titled *Kung Fu: The Return of Caine*, the TV movie produced in the 1980s was eventually called, simply, *Kung Fu: The Movie*. Carradine pitched the idea to Warner Bros. after he appeared on *Saturday Night Live*. During that performance, Carradine did a skit in which he parodied *Kung Fu*. Carradine remembers thinking, "This is an ideal opportunity to find out if I can still play the character, or if it's lost to me, because if it's a comedy and I blow it, it will still be funny."

Carradine wanted to discover if he could still play the character because during his New York visit for *Saturday Night Live*, he met with Radames Pera. The two actors discovered that they both were interested in doing a similar story about Kwai Chang Caine's son. Back in California, Carradine sold Warner Bros. on the idea, and work on *Kung Fu: The Movie* soon began.

One complication, however, was that the sets for the original series had long since been dismantled. The exterior set had been turned into a parking lot. The interior set had been made into a big cave and ship for producer Steven Spielberg's movie *The Goonies*. As a result, the flashbacks for the movie could no longer be shot at the same Shaolin temple. Instead, it was decided that when the foreground story required Caine to consider his masters' wisdom, Caine would talk to the ghost of Master Po.

The movie also differed from the series because it was set in Boston instead of the West, and it took place ten years later than the original series did. That way, for series' viewers, Caine had moved into the future in apparently real time.

Not long after *Kung Fu: The Movie* aired, another pilot idea was submitted to David Carradine. Carradine says he didn't like the script. It seemed to him that the show was going to be about "*kung-fu* car crashes," so he turned it down. The series idea never sold, but the pilot did air. Below are synopses of both projects.

THE MADE-FOR-TV MOVIE OF 1986

Title:	**Kung Fu: The Movie**
Original airdate:	**2-1-86**
Based on a character created by:	**Ed Spielman**
Writer:	**Durrell Royce Crays**
Director:	**Richard Lang**
Producer:	**Skip Ward**
Executive Producer:	**Paul R. Picard**

Years after his initial exile to America, Caine has found a measure of peace in his relationship with a humble Chinese family, headed by "The Old One." As the movie opens, the Old One dies of natural causes and Caine grieves. More sorrow follows: Caine is framed

for the murder of the Reverend
Lawrence Perkins; then he
learns that, in China, all the
Shaolin masters and the original Shaolin temple have been
destroyed. This information
comes to Caine via Chung
Wang, who, it turns out, is
Caine's son by Mayli Ho, a
woman he knew from his days
in China. (See episodes #37 and
#38 of the original series.)
Chung Wang is under the spell
of the evil Royal Chinese
emperor, and the emperor is
out to avenge his nephew's
death at Caine's hands by killing Caine.

The Royal
Chinese Emperor
(Mako) seeks to
avenge his
nephew's murder
by mystically
influencing
Caine's son
(Brandon Lee) to
kill his father, in
Kung Fu: The
Movie.

Meanwhile, Caine begins to
realize that he has feelings for
the preacher's widow, Sarah
Perkins. To complicate matters,
it turns out that Sarah's father
is at the helm of an opium-
smuggling ring. Caine battles
the ringleaders and wins, but
Sarah is killed in the process. Caine is overwhelmed with grief: the
Old One is dead, Master Kan is dead, the Shaolin temple is gone,
and Sarah is lost. In addition, Caine still has one more battle
ahead: he needs to confront the emperor and his entourage. The
showdown is powerful and dramatic, requiring Caine to employ all
of his *kung-fu* skills and much of his intelligence and daring as
well. Caine defeats the emperor's hired assassins and, finally, the
emperor himself. As a result, the dark spell put on Chung Wang is
broken, and Caine is released from the long-standing threat of revenge by the Chinese royal family. As the story closes, Caine
becomes master to his son, who now yearns to learn the way of the
Shaolin.

Notes: The movie opens with a shot of Caine levitating. Of this scene, Radames Pera says, "I think it automatically turned a lot of people off. I mean, I do believe in some supernatural things, but this did not really jibe with the original concept of the show. . . . Caine was a highly trained *human*. He was a counterculture hero. He was antiestablishment. I mean, people cheered for Kwai Chang Caine because he was the underdog and a minority who was slandered and someone who had this incredible personal integrity. And yet he did not flaunt his power."

One of the most satisfying scenes in the film for David Carradine was in the epilogue. Here, the son Chung Wang and the father Caine have a conversation that almost replicates the famous "grasshopper" discussion that the young Caine had with Master Po. In becoming master to his own son,

At the end of Kung Fu: The Movie, Caine and his son are at peace with each other.

Caine becomes more at peace with himself. In the scene, Caine enjoys the irony of the moment and laughs.

The late Brandon Lee, son of Bruce Lee, played Caine's son, Chung Wang. Toward the end of the film, Chung Wang asks Caine if he is his father. The question seems somewhat ironic since—in real life—Brandon's father was the chief contender for the role of Caine in the series. After Bruce Lee lost the part to Carradine, he went back to China, where he made *Enter the Dragon*, the film that began his legendary career in martial arts movies. When Bruce Lee died at age thirty-two, it was under odd circumstances. Some have claimed that he received the "touch of death," a mysterious condition that can supposedly kill an otherwise healthy man by causing him to have an aneurysm. Brandon Lee, like his father, was a popular actor at the time of his death on March 31, 1993, at the age of twenty-eight. At the time, Brandon Lee was filming *The Crow*, an action-adventure film about a murdered rock star who comes back to life with supernatural powers so he can avenge his death. Reportedly, Brandon Lee died twelve hours after an apparent accident on the film set in which a live .44 caliber slug, from a gun presumed to have been rigged to shoot blanks, hit him in the abdomen.

Additional Credits for *Kung Fu: The Movie*

Kwai Chang Caine/Co-Producer	**David Carradine**
Master Po	**Keye Luke**
Chung Wang	**Brandon Lee**
The Emperor	**Mako**
The Old One	**Benson Fong**
Sarah Perkins	**Kerrie Keane**
Sheriff Mills	**Luke Askew**
John Martin Perkins III	**Martin Landau**
Co-starring	**Ellen Geer, Robert Harper, Paul Rudd**
Assistant to the Producers	**Maggie Hepburn**
Director of Photography	**Robert Seaman**
Stunt Coordinator	**Michael Vendrell**

THE NINETY-MINUTE SUMMER MOVIE PILOT OF 1987

Title:	**Kung Fu: The Next Generation**
Original airdate:	**6-19-87**

Based on a character created by: Ed Spielman
Writers: Danny Bilson, Paul De Meo
Director: Tony Wharmby
Producers: Danny Bilson, Paul De Meo
Co-producer: Ralph Riskin
Executive producer: Paul R. Picard

Johnny Caine (Brandon Lee, making his second appearance in the Kung Fu *world) and Kwai Chang Caine (David Darlow, who bears a striking resemblance to David Carradine) in the 1987 made-for-TV movie pilot* Kung Fu: The Next Generation

The story opens on a street in contemporary Bel Air, California. Two men—Johnny and Mick—are preparing to break into a house. Suddenly Johnny decides he doesn't want to go through with the crime. He offers no explanation, but it is clear from the conversation that Mick and Johnny have a history of breaking and entering, and that Johnny has some desire to put his criminal past behind him. Nonetheless, Mick convinces Johnny to do this one last job, so that Levin, the man he works for, will not "come down hard" on Mick for failing to deliver promised goods. The two men skillfully leap over a fence and avoid security alarms, but then Mick's toe grazes the electric eye of a security system. Guards show up. Mick manages to run away, but Johnny is caught and taken to police headquarters. When asked to give his name, Johnny says that he is Kwai Chang Caine.

It turns out that Johnny's great-grandfather is the original Kwai Chang Caine. Johnny shares a name with his great-grandfather and with his father, who is living in contemporary Los Angeles. Johnny's father (who also goes by the name Caine) is an advocate of peace. He lives simply, teaches the virtues of kung-fu, is a merchant of herbs, and offers assistance to those in need. When Johnny shows up at police headquarters, the authorities—as a favor to the man who has been such a helpful public servant—let Johnny go in Caine's custody. Caine apologizes for the behavior of his son, whom he has not seen in a year. He confesses he did not even know he was in the area; then he takes the young man home and sets him up in an austere apartment in his garage. Caine tells his son that he must "settle his debt" with his father. Johnny is confused. "Look," Johnny says, "I've done some stupid things, but back there you said I stole from you. When?"

Caine answers: "You took the knowledge and training I gave you, and used it for evil." Johnny does not deny this, though later he tells his father that he expects, that he has always expected, too much, that he required his son and his apparently estranged wife to be too perfect.

Johnny, though impatient with his father, seems to want to change his life. Caine takes his son for a long drive to the place where the original Kwai Chang Caine supposedly settled down after his years of wanderings. While there, Johnny thinks he sees the ghost of his great grandfather. He appears moved, but then he leaves the site to call Mick to arrange to make another "hit," to help Mick rob a railroad. Before he agrees to do the job, however, Johnny insists on one condition: that he be allowed to meet Levin, the mastermind of all the crimes that Mick has persuaded Johnny to commit.

During the railroad heist, Johnny is shocked to discover that what he is stealing is guns—as opposed to the usual VCRs, TVs, and CD players. Nonetheless, Johnny is still interested in meeting Levin, and he seems to be turning away from the few peaceful habits he was picking up from his father. For instance, he had started to play the flute in the evenings in his garage apartment, but now he goes off to buy a miniature tape player. (Earlier, his father had had his son give all his electronic equipment to the Children's Hospital Thrift Store.)

Finally, Johnny goes with Mick to meet Levin. Johnny's father, Caine—who has been noting his son's late-night departures from the house—secretly trails him. When they get to Levin's warehouse, Johnny discovers there is no Levin. Mick has been the boss of the operation all along. With Mick's henchmen standing all around, Johnny says, "You could've told me . . . But, hey, this is great. We'll be partners, right?"

Mick laughs and says, "You think I'm stupid? First you want out. Then, you get busted. Now you want *in* again, and you're talking 'partners.' Smells like cops to me."

Johnny denies the false charges, but Mick finds the microcassette tape player in Johnny's pocket and is immediately ready to kill his former friend for being a snitch. Just as he is about to kill Johnny, Caine bursts into the room and spills a tall rack laden with electronic equipment. Together, father and son defeat the criminals by using *kung-fu* moves to subdue the unarmed and by using their skills at diving and rolling to hide behind boxes when Uzi machine-gun fire comes their way.

Notes: In the *Kung Fu* series that began in the 1990s (see chapter 11), the character of Caine's grandson is reintroduced, but the other details of *Kung Fu: The Next Generation* were not adopted for the new series. One inconsistency between this movie and the old series is that Caine has a wife. In the series, it was suggested that though Caine could have relations with women, a Shaolin was not to marry. The intriguing detail about Caine's wife (that is, the fact that he had a wife who no longer lives with him—perhaps because he is too much of a perfectionist) is never elaborated on in this movie, though at one point Caine does say to his son, "Maybe I've been too hard on you, but that's because you're all I've got."

In the scene where Johnny and his father go to the original Caine's homestead, we learn that though the original Caine is presumed dead, no one knows the circumstances of his demise. He just happened to disappear from the homestead one day.

Additional Credits for *Kung Fu: The Next Generation*

Kwai Chang Caine	**David Darlow**
Johnny Caine	**Brandon Lee**
Lt. Lois Poole	**Paula Kelley**
Guest Stars	**Miguel Ferrer, Victor Brandt**

Co-stars	Marcia Christie, Dominic Barto, Aaron Heyman, Michael Gilles, Neil Flynn, Mark Everett, Oscar Dillon, Michael Walter, John C. Cooke, Eddie Mack, Richard Duran
Director of Photography	Brianne Murphy

The logo for the new series Kung Fu: The Legend Continues. *The Yin-Yang symbol is used in the Shaolin and other Chinese philosophies.*

KUNG FU
The Legend Continues

CHAPTER ELEVEN

The Legend Continues

IN THE NEW SERIES *Kung Fu: The Legend Continues*, David Carradine plays the character of Caine's grandson. The story takes place in a metropolitan city, somewhere in the United States. (Actual filming is done in Toronto.) The modern-day Caine is, of course, a master of *kung-fu*. His son, Peter, is a police detective, fighting big-city crime. The important people in their lives include Peter's beautiful ex-fiancée and a character called, simply, "the Ancient"—an old Shaolin monk who is the proprietor of an apothecary in the heart of Chinatown.

First broadcast in January 1993, the new, hour-long *Kung Fu* episodes are aired in 225 different markets, through the Prime Time Entertainment Network (PTEN) syndicated package.

THE NEW SERIES

Title:	***Kung Fu: The Legend Continues***
Based on a character created by:	**Ed Spielman**
Pilot story:	**Michael Sloan, Ed Waters**
Pilot teleplay:	**Michael Sloan**
Director:	**Jud Taylor**
Executive producer:	**Michael Sloan**
Supervising producer:	**Maurice Hurley**
Producer:	**Susan Murdoch**
Coproducers:	**Larry LaLonde, Phil Bedard**

Caine (David Carradine) remains a master and a friend to his son Peter (Nathaniel Moreau, above) in the early years and later, when Peter (Chris Potter, next page) is grown up.

Fifteen years ago, Caine, a widower, was raising young Peter alone among a small group of monks in a Shaolin temple he had founded in the American West. The harmony of the temple was shattered when Tan, a renegade monk and sworn enemy of Caine, burned the temple to the ground.

In the aftermath of the fire, Caine believes his young son was killed, and Peter, too, believes his father died in the blaze. It might seem surprising that both men could be so mistaken in their beliefs, but a Shaolin priest—who is also a good friend of the family—created this lie in order to protect the Caines from their unrelenting, deadly enemy Tan.

After the fire, Caine becomes a wanderer, and Peter is cared for by the Shaolin priest until the priest becomes ill. Then, Peter is placed in an orphanage.

Some fifteen years later, Caine's travels bring him to the city where Peter lives and works. Caine wanders into Chinatown and sees two thugs roughing up a Chinese merchant who is refusing to pay protection money. One of the thugs takes out a knife and threatens to peel the merchant's skin like an orange. Caine saves the man and learns from him and others who gather on the street that the neighborhood is in the throes of a battle with a mysterious evil man who wants to control Chinatown. As the residents complain and worry, Marilyn, the mayor's assistant, tries to encourage people not to become violent vigilantes, to go through legal channels to improve their situation.

Meanwhile, Peter, an untraditional, somewhat playful, police-man, convinces his boss to let him go undercover as an assassin for the mysterious crime lord.

Father and son are reunited as they become further involved in fighting the mysterious gangster, who turns out to be none other than Tan. More coincidences and surprises follow. The Ancient, the kindly apothecary whom the people of Chinatown turn to for support—moral and otherwise—in their fight against Tan, bears a striking resemblance to the Shaolin priest who, years ago, sepa-rated Caine and Peter with his well-intentioned lie. Marilyn—who appeared to be trying to help the people of Chinatown—is really Tan's lover.

Marilyn stumbles onto Peter's true identity and reveals the secret to an already suspicious Tan. Tan tries to kill his old foe, and in a dramatic finale, both father and son fight the evil man. In the midst of the combat, Peter turns breathlessly to his father and says, "Ever thought of joining the police force? You kick 'em, I'll shoot 'em, this is one hell of a team." Though Peter is barely conscious by the end of the fight, he and his father defeat Tan.

At the close of the ninety-minute pilot of the new series, Caine is persuaded to stop his wanderings and stay in the city. In subsequent episodes, parent and son continue to realize how different they are. Caine lives his belief that violence must be avoided. For Peter, violence is a way of life and force a real necessity. Nonetheless, as their relationship develops, Peter turns to his father for help with his cases. The two deal with a white slavery ring, tense hos-tage situations, and murderers. As the bond between the two

Caine disposes of an adversary in the pilot for the new series Kung Fu: The Legend Continues *(1992).*

grows stronger, Peter finds himself recalling his early years at the Shaolin temple out west; increasingly, he draws upon Caine's wisdom and mystical powers. At the same time, Caine struggles to adapt to his disturbing surroundings in the violent city and to his reborn fatherhood.

Notes: The identity of the modern-day Caine in this new series is, according to Carradine, "sort of a secret." Although the character in the new series refers to the original Caine as "my grandfather," some people working on the shows are of the opinion that the current Caine is not a descendant of the original Caine but the same man. Carradine explains: "It is documented that one *kung-fu* master—who was also a nutritionist and whose formulas I take—lived to be 253 years old. . . . Of course, documentation in China is different from what American documentation is."

In general, however, the new series tries to avoid plot situations and characters that are absolutely unbelievable. Carradine says: "Like when they want me to jump twenty feet up onto a roof? I say, 'Look, this is like the old Chinese movies. This is not what we're doing here. Everything that this new Caine does should be possible. Somebody should think it's possible.'"

Interestingly enough, Kim Chan, who plays the Ancient in the new series, is, in fact, a Shaolin master. He was, Carradine says, "hired because he gave a good reading . . . and it was only after we were on the set that we found out he was the real thing . . . which we had never had before."

Left to right: *Peter (Chris Potter), the Ancient (Kim Chan), and Caine (David Carradine) in a scene from* Kung Fu: The Legend Continues

Additional Credits for *Kung Fu: The Legend Continues*

Kwai Chang Caine/Coproducer	**David Carradine**
Peter Caine	**Chris Potter**
Lt. Paul Blaisdell	**Robert Lansing**
The Ancient	**Kim Chan**
Frank Strenlich	**William Dunlop**
Tyler Smith	**Marla Schaffel**
Young Peter	**Nathaniel Moreau**
Narrator	**Richard Anderson**
Guest stars	**Ernest Abuba, Lori Hallier, Mark W. Conklin, Tom Matsusaka, Don Allison, Allan Tong, Von Flores**
Co-stars	**Kevin Jubinville, Harvey Chao, Bernadette Li, Matt Trueman, David Chant, Harvey Sololoff, Ardon Bess, Diane Douglas, Alice Poon, Ho Chow, Margaret Man**
Executive in Charge of Production	**Nigel Watts**
Associate Producer	**Bernadette Joyce**
Director of Photography	**Laszlo George**
Fight Choreographer/ Technical Adviser	**Michael Vendrell**
Stunt Coordinator	**Branko Racki**

APPENDIXES

The journey does not end. It continues, from one time to another.

KWAI CHANG CAINE, *Episode #5, "The Soul is a Warrior"*

Selected Biographies

DAVID CARRADINE (b. 1936)

Kwai Chang Caine

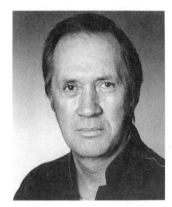

Son of actor John Carradine, David Carradine was born in Hollywood and brought up in California, New York, Massachusetts, and Vermont. After his years in school and in the army, he landed starring roles in two Broadway plays—*The Deputy* and *The Royal Hunt of the Sun*. He then went to Hollywood to act in the short-lived TV series Shane and in other films. All this work led to his starring role in *Kung Fu*, starting in 1972. During this period, Carradine became romantically involved with actress Barbara Hershey, and the two had a son named Free.

After the end of the original *Kung Fu* series, Carradine devoted himself primarily to his film career. He has had roles in *The Serpent's Egg*, *Boxcar Bertha*, *Mean Streets*, *Bound for Glory*, and *Roadside Warriors*, among other films.

Today, besides acting in the new *Kung Fu* series, Carradine seriously pursues his interest in music, composing, sculpting, and painting. He is the author of a book on *kung-fu* philosophy titled *The Spirit of Shaolin* (Boston: Charles Tuttle, 1991). He has also made two videos: *David Carradine's Kung Fu Workout* (Time-Life, 1991) and *David Carradine's Tai Chi Workout* (Time-Life, 1991).

Currently, Carradine and Gail Jensen, his third wife and his manager, live in Ontario next to an apple orchard. They also maintain a horse ranch in the mountains north of Los Angeles.

Carradine's daughter, Calista, twenty-five, is acting in the new *Kung Fu* series. She has given David two granddaughters: Mariah and Sienna. David's son Free, nineteen, is studying astronomy in college; and his youngest, Kansas, fourteen, is a horse enthusiast.

KEYE LUKE (1904–1991)
Master Po

Keye Luke started his Hollywood career in the art department of Twentieth Century–Fox. He was quickly drawn away to acting, however, once he was encouraged to take a role in *The Painted Veil*, starring Greta Garbo.

Luke first became known to the public as Charlie Chan's Number One Son in the *Charlie Chan* movie series. He played regular roles on several TV series, including *General Hospital* and *Sidekicks*. He also did numerous television guest appearances and commercials. His film work included roles in *Gremlins*, *Project X*, *The Hawaiians*, and *Alice*.

PHILIP AHN (1905–1978)
Master Kan

Born in Los Angeles, Philip Ahn attended area public schools and then studied at the University of Southern California. His career in film and television began in 1936. While he was still a student at USC, he was picked for a role in the movie *Anything Goes*, starring Bing Crosby.

Ahn's later film work included roles in *The General Died at Dawn*, *Disputed Passage*, *Stowaway*, *The Left Hand of God*, *Impact*, *Thoroughly Modern Millie*, and *Jonathan Livingston Seagull*. He made appearances on many TV shows, including *M*A*S*H*, *Mr. Garland*, and *Love, American Style*.

Ahn's father, Chang Ho Ahn, was one of the original founders of the Republic of Korea. In the early 1970s, the younger Ahn attended a special dedication ceremony in Seoul, during which the government honored his dead father by naming a memorial park and a Seoul street in his honor. At the time of his death in 1978, Philip Ahn was planning to go to Korea to work on a film documentary about his father's efforts for freedom during the Japanese occupation of his homeland.

RADAMES PERA (b. 1960)
Young Caine (Grasshopper)

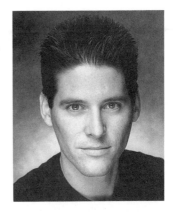

Radames Pera was born in New York City to an Uruguayan artist and a Russian aspiring actress and model. The marriage did not last, and Pera's mother decided to pursue an acting career in Hollywood. She moved to the West Coast in 1964 and landed a few guest-starring roles on TV and in films. Then, in the fall of 1967, she was up for a role opposite Anthony Quinn in a feature film to be directed by Daniel Mann. Radames Pera's chance meeting with the director led to a screen test and, eventually, the role of the son in the film *A Dream of Kings*.

At eleven, Pera landed the role of Grasshopper in the original *Kung Fu* series. Pera had originally told his mother he wanted to act for only a few years, but at age thirteen, in the midst of a successful TV series, he was the family's sole support, and he was persuaded by his mother to keep acting.

When the first *Kung Fu* series ended, Pera was cast in a recurring role as John Junior, the character Mary Ingalls's love interest on TV's *Little House on the Prairie*.

In the fall of 1978, Pera decided to follow his acting teacher, Stella Adler, to New York, to attend her classes. Three years later, he returned to Los Angeles. Although he picked up some roles, Pera's acting career never quite resumed full force. Eventually, he decided to abandon his plan to use acting as a path to directing. Instead, he began experimenting with video technology and its artistic possibilities.

During this time, he met his wife, Marsha Mann, a singer, songwriter, producer, and threatrical director. The two were married five thousand feet above the Mojave Desert on Leap Year Day in 1984. After exchanging rings and vows, they skydived out of a plane. They called the event "A Leap of Faith."

The further Radames got from acting, the better he felt, so in 1988, with his newly acquired skills, he started his own business —All Systems Go!—which designs and installs audio/video systems and home theaters. Pera's clients include Nicholas Cage, Robert Downey, Jr., Johnny Depp, Sharon Stone, Winona Ryder, Chuck Norris, and many Hollywood producers and directors.

JAMES HONG

Various guest-starring roles

James Hong grew up in Minneapolis's Chinatown, where his father operated a nightclub and several restaurants. His father sent the entire family to Hong Kong for an early Chinese education. When World War II broke out, they caught one of the last boats back to America.

As a young man, Hong studied civil engineering. After his schooling, he chose to make his home on the West Coast. As a contestant on Groucho Marx's quiz show *You Bet Your Life*, Hong impersonated Marx and subsequently won a nightclub contract. Eventually, Hong left his LA County engineering job to act in the film *Love Is a Many-Splendored Thing*.

Hong's other film credits include *Big Trouble in Little China*, *Nerds in Paradise*, *Blade Runner*, *Black Widow*, *The In-Laws*, *Chinatown*, and *Missing in Action*.

Hong has actively fought for the rights of Asian-American actors. He was president of the Association of Asian/Pacific American Artists and remains a charter member.

BEULAH QUO

Various guest-starring roles

As a Phi Beta Kappa with a degree in sociology, Beulah Quo had no intention of going into movie acting, but an interview with the director of *Love Is a Many-Splendored Thing* landed her her first role. Since then, she has appeared in the films *Flower Drum Song*, *The Sand Pebbles*, and *Chinatown*. She also has played a recurring role on the daytime TV soap opera *General Hospital*, among numerous other parts.

Beulah Quo is a committed public servant. Among other projects, she has been involved in the Association of Asian/Pacific American Artists; served as vice-president of the United Way's Region V board of directors; and worked as a board member for the China Society, the oldest Chinese-American cultural/educational organization in the United States.

SOON-TECK OH
Various guest-starring roles

Soon-Teck Oh is a martial artist, equally familiar with the languages and customs of Japan, China, and Korea. He is also a writer, and some of his theatrical work has been produced by Los Angeles's East-West Players.

On Broadway, Soon-Teck Oh has performed in *Pacific Overtures*. Elsewhere, he acted in *Ghost, Hamlet, Romeo and Juliet, No Exit*, and *Rashomon*. His recent films are *Missing in Action II, Steele Justice, Death Wish 4*, and *Collision Course*. He is often remembered for his portrayal of Lieutenant Hip in the James Bond movie *The Man with the Golden Gun*.

MAKO
Various guest-starring roles

Mako (aka Makoto Iwamatsu) was born in the seaport of Kobe, Japan. He came to the United States in his early teens. In the late 1940s, he began studying architecture. Within a year or two, friends got him involved in designing theater lights, sets, and props. Soon, he had a desire to act as well. He had his first professional instruction at the Pratt Institute in New York. Then, he made the West Coast his home.

In Hollywood, Mako worked on a number of disappointing television shows. This helped form his belief that a special medium was needed for Asian-American actors to perfect and display their craft. In 1965, he helped found the East-West Players, and he is currently the producing artistic director of the LA company.

His most recent stage credit is the Circle in the Square's production of *The King and I* at the Minneapolis Opera House. His most recent film credits include *Tucker* and *The Wash*.

BENSON FONG (1916–1987)
Various guest-starring roles

In 1943, while working as a grocery store operator in Sacramento, California, Benson Fong was discovered by a Paramount Pictures executive who appoached him in a restaurant and asked him if he would like to be in the movies.

Fong appeared in numerous plays and television films. His screen credits include *China, Behind the Rising Sun, Calcutta, The Love Bug,* and *The Strongest Man in the World.*

Fong also owned five Ah Fong's restaurants in the Los Angeles area.

RICHARD LOO (1903-1983)
Various guest-starring roles

Born in Hawaii, Richard Loo had roles in many films, including *The Good Earth, The Purple Heart, The Man With the Golden Gun, Five Fingers, Soldier of Fortune,* and *A Girl Named Tamiko.* He regularly appeared in TV situation comedies, including *Bewitched, My Three Sons,* and *I Dream of Jeannie.*

VICTOR-SEN YUNG (1915-1980)

Various guest-starring roles

Victor-Sen Yung's parents left China at the end of the nine-teenth century. Born Sen Yung in San Francisco in 1915, Yung landed his first movie role as an extra in *The Good Earth*. Around the same time, he was employed as a salesman for a chemical company. Officially, his career in film began when he tried to attract Twentieth Century–Fox technicians to his company's flameproofing material. At that time, he was of-fered a part in the *Charlie Chan* movie series.

From then on, Yung worked consistently in Hollywood—save for the war years, when he was a captain in Air Force In-telligence.

His credits include *Forbidden*, *Blood Alley*, and *The Man with Bogart's Face*. He was a regular on the TV show *Bachelor Father* and he played the cook Hop Sing on *Bonanza*.

Long after all three of the series he worked on had gone into syndication, Yung was earning his livelihood primarily from his culinary skills. He wrote *The Great Wok Cookbook* (Los Angeles: Nash, 1974). In 1980, he was working on his sec-ond cookbook when he was found dead in his small San Fer-nando Valley bungalow. He had been asphyxiated by gas fumes from his kitchen stove.

ROBERT ITO

Various guest-starring roles

Robert Ito began his career in the entertainment industry as a dancer with the National Ballet of Canada. Since moving to Los Angeles, in 1965, he has made countless film and televi-sion appearances. He is best known for the role of Sam Fuji-yama on *Quincy*.

Like many of his *Kung Fu* colleagues, Ito has been associ-ated with the East-West Players in Los Angeles since the group began in 1965.

MICHAEL GREENE

Various guest-starring roles

Michael Greene has performed in over one hundred television shows and numerous movies. His film credits include *Moon Over Parador, Less Than Zero, Down and Out in Beverly Hills, Moscow on the Hudson, Lost in America,* and *Naked Angels.*

DAVID CHOW (b. 1936)

Technical adviser; occasional guest-starring roles

At the age of fourteen, Chow Tai-Wai left Shanghai for Hong Kong with a modest sum in US dollars—a gift from his father. In the course of several months, the teenager made careful investments and increased his funds by over 700 percent.

Then, Chow Tai-Wai, now David Chow, emigrated—completely alone—to America. Instead of enrolling in high school, he took the College Board exams with 320 adult applicants and was one of 9 people who passed. This earned him admission to UCLA. After being graduated at the age of seventeen, he went on to earn his master's in economics at the University of Southern California.

Chow quickly put his business skills to work and was able to retire at the age of twenty-seven. Chow then had the leisure to develop his interests, and, he reports, his strongest interest was—and is—helping his fellow man. He established one of the first air- and water-pollution-control companies in the United States and one of the first personal-computer firms.

As an actor, Chow performed in many television shows (including *Mannix, The Dean Martin Show,* and *Days of Our Lives)* and movies (such as *Planet of the Apes, The Girl Who Knew Too Much,* and *Skin Game).* He is also the author of the book *Kung-Fu: History, Philosophy, and Techniques* (Unique Publications, 1980).

Among other activities, he currently teaches martial arts and volunteers for the Los Angeles County Sheriff's Department.

KAM YUEN (b. 1941)
Technical adviser; occasional guest-starring roles

Originally from Hong Kong, Kam Yuen moved to Manhattan when he was young. He was graduated from Manhattan College with a degree in engineering, and he worked as a research-and-development engineer for many years.

Today, Kam Yuen is the chief instructor, chiropractor, nutritionist, and Chinese herbalist at Shaolin West in Woodland Hills, California. He has authored two books: *Beginning Kung Fu* (Ohara Publications, 1975) and *Technique and Form of the Three-Sectional Staff* (Ohara Publications, 1979).

In addition to being David Carradine's personal *kung-fu* instructor, Kam Yuen has been the martial arts teacher for celebrities such as Tony Danza, Bob Dylan, Michael Jackson, Chuck Norris, and Barbara Hershey.

GUY LEE
Talent agent

Guy Lee heads the Guy Lee and Associates talent agency. Through this agency, he has helped establish the acting careers of hundreds of Asian actors.

Lee's own acting career started when he was five and performing in vaudeville. He went on to film work with all the major studios, including roles in *Hong Kong* with Ronald Reagan, *Never So Few* with Frank Sinatra, and *Blue Hawaii* with Elvis Presley.

Lee has also worked in the theater and on television. He helped establish the East-West Players. In 1973, he became a partner with Bessie Loo, of the Bessie Loo Agency. Two years later, he assumed full control of the company.

ED SPIELMAN

Cocreator of pilot for original series

Ed Spielman is credited with having created the television series which sparked the kung fu craze of the 1970s and the resultant world-wide martial arts boom. In his career, Spielman has worked for every major motion picture studio and television network. As screenwriter and producer, in addition to *Kung Fu*, Spielman created the Disney/ABC miniseries *Earth Star Voyager* and the ABC series *The Young Riders*, for which he won the Western Heritage "Wrangler" Award. He began his career as a page at ABC-TV in New York, while attending Brooklyn College where he studied television production. Spielman has authored the biography *The Mighty Atom*, which, when published by Viking Press, was honored by the American Library Association as one of the best books of the year. Spielman currently works as an executive producer and writer with his brother Howard Spielman.

HOWARD FRIEDLANDER (b. 1947)

Cocreator of pilot for original series

After working his way through school as a page for ABC and then CBS, Howard Friedlander departed from New York University with a bachelor's degree in film and television production.

After his *Kung Fu* success, Friedlander wrote several more screenplays with Ed Spielman, including *Gordon's War* and *The Moonbeam Riders*. Then, Spielman and Friedlander parted amicably, and Friedlander started working with Ken Peragine. Together, they wrote episodes of *The Bob Newhart Show*, *Cheers*, and *O'Hara*. They also developed and wrote projects for Walt Disney Pictures.

Along with his screenwriting career, Friedlander spent several years as the head writer and creative consultant for the award-winning children's television series *Captain Kangaroo*.

JERRY THORPE

First-season producer; second- and third-season executive producer; director

Son of director Richard Thorpe, Jerry Thorpe succeeded in the movie business without help from his father, who had encouraged his son to try a more secure profession. After a brief stint—during and after high school—with ice-skating shows and as an ice hockey player, Thorpe went to work as a clerk-typist for MGM's production department. He worked his way up to apprentice script supervisor, then second assistant director, then first. Thorpe worked principally with directors John Sturges and Vincente Minnelli. During production of Minnelli's *The Long, Long Trailer*, starring Lucille Ball and Desi Arnaz, Arnaz offered Thorpe a job and promised him he would be directing within six months if he joined the Desilu Productions team. True enough, with Desilu, Thorpe was soon directing and, over the course of his tenure with Desilu, he directed 110 episodes of *December Bride* and many episodes of *I Love Lucy*. Eventually, Thorpe was named Desilu's vice-president in charge of production and programming. When Lucy and Desi divorced, Thorpe went on to free-lance work before producing *Kung Fu*.

HERMAN MILLER

Second- and third-season producer; developer of pilot; writer
Herman Miller has produced many television shows, including *Cannon*, *Houston Knights*, and *Man from Atlantis*. He created *McCloud*; served as executive script consultant for *The New Mike Hammer* series; and wrote episodes of *Knight Rider*, *MacGyver*, and *Hunter*.

JOHN FURIA, JR.

First-season story consultant and writer; second-season producer and story consultant

In 1950, John Furia, Jr., was graduated from Fordham University with a double major in philosophy and constitutional history. Since then, he has amassed a long list of professional credits. He has worked both as a writer and producer on the television series *John O'Hara's Gibbsville*, *Apple's Way*, and *Insight*. He has written for many other shows, including *Bonanza* and *The Waltons*.

Furia has been associated with the Writers Guild of America West in a number of capacities over the past thirty years. At various times, he has been chairman, president, and chair of the Constitutional Review Committee, among other positions.

For the Academy of Television Arts and Sciences, he has served as secretary, as well as on the board of directors. He has also been a consultant for the National Endowment for the Humanites.

Today, while still involved in all phases of the entertainment industry, Furia is director of the film-writing program at the University of Southern California. He is a professor at USC and lectures widely on writing for film.

ALEX BEATON

First-season associate producer; second- and third-season producer; director

To put himself through school, Alex Beaton submitted applications for employment at an investment firm, a supermarket, and all the major motion picture companies. Three days after he applied to Twentieth Century–Fox, he was hired for an opening in the mailroom. He worked his way up to the research department, then moved to MGM Studios when a position in the apprentice film editor program became available. He went on to become an assistant editor, then a film editor, then an associate producer, and finally a producer for *Kung Fu*.

A partial list of the television shows that he has produced includes *Harry O.*, *The Greatest American Hero*, and *Wiseguy*.

JOHN BADHAM

Director

Born in England to an actress and a US army general, John Badham moved to the United States when his father was transferred to Alabama. Badham's sister, Mary, became the first of two siblings to break into the movie business when, at the age of ten, she received a 1962 Oscar nomination for her role in *To Kill a Mockingbird*.

Badham did undergraduate work in philosophy, then entered the Yale School of Drama. Inspired by his sister's early success, he went to Hollywood and landed a job in the mailroom of Universal Studios. He worked his way up through the ranks, steadily learning all he could about directing.

Badham is responsible for the direction in a number of popular films, including *Bird on a Wire*, *The Hard Way*, *War Games*, *American Flyers*, *Short Circuit*, and *Saturday Night Fever*.

Emmy Nominations and Awards

1972

FRANK C. WESTMORE, Makeup, *Kung Fu: The Pilot*
OUTSTANDING ACHIEVEMENT IN MAKEUP—single program or a series or a special program (Nomination)

1973

JACK WOOLF, Cinematographer, Episode #4, "An Eye for an Eye"
OUTSTANDING ACHIEVEMENT IN CINEMATOGRAPHY FOR ENTERTAINMENT PROGRAMMING (Award)

JERRY THORPE, Director, Episode #4, "An Eye for an Eye"
OUTSTANDING DIRECTORIAL ACHIEVEMENT IN DRAMA—single program or a series without continuing characters (Award)

FRANK C. WESTMORE, Makeup, Episode #11, "Chains"
OUTSTANDING ACHIEVEMENT IN MAKEUP—single program or a series or a special program (Nomination)

MICHAEL GREENE, Episode #11, "Chains"
OUTSTANDING SINGLE PERFORMANCE BY A SUPPORTING ACTOR IN A COMEDY OR DRAMA SERIES (Nomination)

DAVID CARRADINE
OUTSTANDING CONTINUED PERFORMANCE BY AN ACTOR IN A LEADING ROLE (Nomination)

JERRY THORPE, Producer
OUTSTANDING NEW SERIES (Nomination)

JERRY THORPE, PRODUCER
OUTSTANDING DRAMA SERIES—CONTINUING (Nomination)

1974
LEW AYRES, Episode #44, "The Vanishing Image"
OUTSTANDING SINGLE PERFORMANCE BY A SUPPORTING ACTOR IN A COMEDY
OR A DRAMA SERIES (Nomination)

Sample Shooting Schedule

Reproduced on the following several pages, in its entirety, is the Warner Bros. Television shooting schedule for *Kung Fu* Episode #30 (described in Chapter 8). The schedule gives fans a behind-the-scenes glimpse at the complexities involved in coordinating the making of a *Kung Fu* show: the actors and crew worked on a tight, highly organized timetable; scenes were shot out of sequence for economy; stunt doubles, extras, animal handlers, enhanced camera apparatus, special effects, postproduction technical work (for the underwater scenes), and other embellishments were required to render the spirit of the story.

December 11, 1973

WARNER BROS. TELEVISION

SHOOTING SCHEDULE

"KUNG FU" TV SERIES

PROD. #166215 "THE RAIDERS"
DAYS ALLOTTED: 7
START DATE: DEC. 12, 1973
FINISH DATE: DEC. 20, 1973

EXEC. PROD: JERRY THORPE
PRODUCERS: A.BEATON/J.FURIA, JR.
DIRECTOR: LEE PHILIPS
UNIT MANAGER: AUSTEN JEWELL
ASST. DIRECTOR: JERRY ZIESMER

DAY/DATE	SET/SCENES	CAST/ATMOS.	LOCATION
1ST DAY WEDNESDAY 12/12/73	EXT. ROAD (D) Scs. 1, 6, 7, 8, 9, 10, 11, 12, 13, 14, 15, 16, 17, 18, 19, 20, 21, 22, 23, 24, 25, 26, 27, 28, 29, 30, 31, 32, 33, 34, 35, 36. 4 2/8 pgs. Robbery. CAMERA: SHORT POINTED #1 STAR FILTER. CONST. FILL LAKE AT SUSPENSION BRIDGE	CAINE HILLQUIST MAULPEDE SARNICKY CAPT. LEE QUOY CHU ST. DBL. CAPT. LEE " " HILLQUIST ATMOS. DRIVER SP. EFX. SHATTER RIFLE STOCK SHOOT OFF LOCK LIVESTOCK & VEH. MINING WAGON 2-UP 2-HORSES 3-ND HORSES	FOX RANCH (SUSPENSION BRIDGE AREA)
	EXT. BRIDGE & TREE (D) Scs. 50, 51, 52, 53, 54, 55, 56, 60, 61, 62, 63, 64. 5 4/8 pgs. (Possible 84A & 115) Treat Chu - Caine leaves.	CAINE CAPT. LEE CHU QUOY SP. EFX. BREAK LIMB LIVESTOCK & VEH. 3-ND HORSES 1-HILLQUIST'S HORSE	

"KUNG FU" - PROD. #166215   SHOOTING SCHEDULE

DAY/DATE	SET/SCENES	CAST/ATMOS.	LOCATION
1ST DAY **WEDNESDAY** 12/12/73 (Continued)	<u>INT. MINING WAGON</u> (D) <u>Scs. 2, 3, 4, 5,</u> 4/8 pg. See Caine. CAMERA: DYNA LENS TITAN: PRE-RIG TO PULL WAGON.	HILLQUIST	FOX RANCH (SUSPENSION BRIDGE AREA)

END OF 1ST DAY - **TOTAL PAGES 10 2/8**

DAY/DATE	SET/SCENES	CAST/ATMOS.	LOCATION

2ND DAY
THURSDAY
12/13/73
	<u>EXT. FARMHOUSE</u> (D)
	Scs. 171, 172, 173, 174,
	   175, 176, 177, 181,
	   182, 183, 185, 186,
	   192pt, 200, 201, 208,
	   209, 210, 211, 212, 213,
	   215, 216, 219, 220, 237,
	   238, 252pt, 253pt, 261,
	   262, 263.
	5 2/8 pgs.
	
	Ambush-Roof-Tag.
	
	TITAN W/POST & RISERS &
	    EXTENSION.
	
	1-ADD'L. CAMERA OPERATOR
	1- " " ASST.
	
	PRE-SET FALL PAD.
		CAINE
		HOYLE
		MEG
		CAPT. LEE
		CHU
		QUOY
		HILLQUIST (Sc. 181)
		MAULPEDE (Sc. 181)
		SARNICKY (Sc. 181)
		SHERIFF (Sc. 219)
		
		<u>ST. DBL.</u>
		CAINE
		SARNICKY
		
		<u>ATMOS.</u>
		7-VIGILANTIES
		3-DEPUTIES (Sc. 219)
		
		<u>SP. EFX.</u>
		1-WATER WAGON
		BULLET EFFECTS-PELLETS
		TORCH
		RIG OF PRAC. RIFLE TO CAMERA
		
		<u>LIVESTOCK & VEH.</u>
		3-HORSES (Sc. 171)
		4-MORE HORSES (Sc. 219)
		3-MORE HORSES (Sc. 253)
			FOX RANCH
			(HUNTER RANCH
			FARMHOUSE)

"KUNG FU" - PROD. #166215   SHOOTING SCHEDULE

DAY/DATE	SET/SCENES	CAST/ATMOS.	LOCATION
2ND DAY THURSDAY 12/13/73 (Continued)	EXT. BARN (D) Scs. 147pt, 154pt, 155, 156, 157, 158, 159, 160, 161, 162. 7/8 pg. This is beauty. TITAN	CAINE QUOY CAPT. LEE CHU LIVESTOCK & VEH. 4-COWS 3-GOATS 10-CHICKENS 3-HORSES 1-WORKHORSE (INCL. BABY ANIMALS)	FOX RANCH (HUNTER RANCH FARMHOUSE)
	EXT. FARM (D) Scs. 138, 139, 144. 7/8 pg. Going to barn.	CAPT. LEE CHU CAINE (Sc. 142) QUOY (Sc. 142) LIVESTOCK & VEH. AS ABOVE	
	INT. BARN (D) Scs. 145, 146, 147pt, 148, 154pt. 1 2/8 pgs. Help chicks.	CAINE QUOY CAPT. LEE LIVESTOCK & VEH. 8-CHICKS	

END OF 2ND DAY - TOTAL PAGES 8 2/8

3RD DAY FRIDAY 12/14/73	INT. FARMHOUSE (D) Scs. 140, 141, 178, 179, 180, 184, 191, 192pt, 193, 194, 195, 202, 203, 204, 205, 206, 207, 214, 217, 218, 219, 220, 221, 222, 223, 224pt, 253pt, 254, 255, 256, 257, 258. 6 pgs. Up to fight & Tag.	CAINE HOYLE MEG CAPT. LEE CHU QUOY SHERIFF (Sc. 253) SP. EFX. BULLET EFFECTS	STAGE 16

END OF 3RD DAY - TOTAL PAGES 6

"KUNG FU" - PROD. #166215   SHOOTING SCHEDULE

DAY/DATE	SET/SCENES	CAST/ATMOS.	LOCATION

SATURDAY 12/15/73 - OFF

SUNDAY 12/16/73 - OFF

DAY/DATE	SET/SCENES	CAST/ATMOS.	LOCATION
4TH & 5TH DAYS MONDAY & TUESDAY 12/17/73 & 12/18/73 NOTE: REHEARSAL STAGE #16 INT. FARMHOUSE FIGHT.	EXT. FOREST CLEARING (D) Scs. 75, 76, 77, 78, 79, 80, 81, 82, 83, 84, 84A, 85, 86, 87, 88, 89, 90, 91, 92, 93, 94, 107, 108, 109, 110, 111, 112, 113, 114, 115, 116, 117, 120, 121, 123, 127, 129, 130, 131, 132, 133, 134, 135, 136. 9 2/8 pgs. Caine put under water. CONST. TREE STUMP	CAINE HOYLE HILLQUIST (Sc. 84A) MAULPEDE (Sc. 84A) SARNICKY (Sc. 84A) CAPT. LEE (Sc. 115) CHU (Sc. 115) QUOY (Sc. 84A) STUNT DBL. CAINE SARNICKY MAULPEDE LIVESTOCK & VEH. 1-WORKHORSE 6-ND HORSES 1-ND WAGON (FARM)	TBS LOT (JUNGLE-LAKE AREA & LARAMIE ST.)

| | EXT. MINING TOWN (D)
Scs. 65, 66, 67, 68.
3/8 pg.

Enter.

LIVESTOCK & VEH.
MINING WAGON 2-UP
2-ND 2-UPS
3-ND HORSES
1-MULE | HILLQUIST
SHERIFF
SARNICKY
MAULPEDE

ATMOS.
18-TOWNSMEN
 1-DRIVER
 1-BARBER
20 | |

| | INT. SALOON (D)
Scs. 69, 70.
2 pgs.

The law will decide. | HILLQUIST
DRIVER
GUARD
SHERIFF
SARNICKY
MAULPEDE

ATMOS.
12-TOWNSMEN
 1-BARBER
 1-DRIVER | |

"KUNG FU" - PROD. #166215   SHOOTING SCHEDULE

DAY/DATE	SET/SCENES	CAST/ATMOS.	LOCATION
4TH & 5TH DAYS MONDAY & TUESDAY 12/17/73 & 12/18/73	INT. SALOON (N) Scs. 163, 165. 6/8 pg. Hire posse.	HILLQUIST SARNICKY MAULPEDE 1ST MINER ATMOS. 18-MEN 1-DRIVER 1-BARBER 20	TBS LOT (JUNGLE-LAKE AREA & LARAMIE ST.)
	EXT. SHERIFF'S OFFICE (N) Scs. 166, 167. 3/8 pg. Thinking.	SHERIFF DEPUTY	

END OF 4TH & 5TH DAYS - TOTAL PAGES 12 6/8

6TH DAY
WEDNESDAY
12/19/73
	INT. FARMHOUSE (D)
	Scs. 224pt, 225, 226, 227,
	       228, 229, 230, 231,
	       232, 233, 234, 235,
	       236, 239, 240, 241,
	       242, 243, 244, 245,
	       246, 247, 248, 249,
	       250, 252, 252.
	3 2/8 pgs.
	
	Fight.
	
	1-HELMET CAMERA (W/20mm PRIME)
	1-MARK II 120 FPS
	1-ARRI
	1-PSR
	1-ARRI BL.
	1-ADDL. CAMERA OPERATOR & ASST.
		CAINE
		HOYLE
		MEG
		CAPT. LEE
		CHU
		QUOY
		
		STUNT DBL.
		CAINE
		CAPT. LEE
		
		SP. EFX.
		COLLAPSABLES & BREAKAWAYS
		
		CONST.
		CEILING PIECES-TEXTURED
			STAGE 16

END OF 6TH DAY - TOTAL PAGES 3 2/8

"KUNG FU" - PROD. #166215   SHOOTING SCHEDULE

DAY/DATE	SET/SCENES	CAST/ATMOS.	LOCATION
7TH DAY **THURSDAY** **12/20/73**	FLASHBACK INT. TEMPLE (D) Scs. 57, 58, 59. 1 1/8 pgs.	YOUNG CAINE MASTER KAN	TBS LOT (CASTLE SET)
	Seek Love.	2-KUNG FU STUNTMEN	
		ATMOS. 1-KUNG FU MASTER	
	2-CAMERA OPERATORS 3- " ASSISTANTS 1-MARK II 120 FPS	SP. EFX. GROTTO & LION FOUNTAINS WORK	
	NIKE		
	INT. TEMPLE (D) Scs. 96, 97, 98, 99, 100, 101, 102, 103, 104. 2 5/8 pgs.	YOUNG CAINE MASTER PO	
	Destroy vases.	SP. EFX. SHATTER VASES (5)	
	INT./EXT. TEMPLE (D) Scs. 149, 150, 151, 152, 153. 1 2/8 pgs.	DISCIPLE CAINE STUDENT	
	Help student.		

END OF 7TH DAY - TOTAL PAGES 5

NOTE:
UNDERWATER SEQUENCE
TO BE SHOT POST PRODUCTION

	EXT. UNDERWATER (D) Scs. 118, 119, 122, 124. 4/8 pg.	CAINE	
	Trapped.	ST. DBL. CAINE	

Index

Abuba, Ernest, 167
Adderley, Julian, 145, 146
Ahn, Philip, 4, 18, 20, 22–23, 43, 60, 61. *See also* Kan, Master
  biography, 172–173
  personality of, 40–42
Ahn, Ralph, 41
Aidman, Charles, 147
Albert, Eddie, 132
Alden, Norm, 80
"Alethea," 81–83
Allen, TaRonce, 93
Allison, Don, 167
"Ambush," 147–148
"Ancient Warrior, The," 89–90
Anderson, John, 69, 113
Anderson, Richard, 167
Apstein, Theodore, 137, 142
"Arrogant Dragon, The," 117
Askew, Luke, 157
"Assassin, The," 94–96
Atwater, Barry, 112
Aubuchon, Jacques, 150
Ayres, Lew, 130, 185

Badham, John, 81, 83
  biography, 183
  on David Carradine, 33

on visual effects, 49
Bakey, Ed, 119, 121
"Barbary House," 148
Barnes, Rayford, 112
Barnes, Walter, 106
Barrymore, John Blyth, 148, 150
Barrymore, John Drew, 109
Barto, Dominic, 161
Barton, Kittridge, 93
"Battle Hymn," 145–146
Beaton, Alex, 44, 58, 61, 147
  biography, 182
  on Caine's character, 30
  on David Carradine, 33–34
  on fights, 49
  on *Kung Fu* style, 9
  on props, 48
  on second-season changes, 123
Beir, Fred, 88
Bellini, Cal, 130
"Besieged"
  "Part 1: Death on Cold Mountain," 138–140
  "Part 2: Cannon at the Gates," 140
Bess, Ardon, 167
Bieri, Ramon, 101
Bilson, Danny, 158
Bishop, Larry, 83

Bishop, Ron, 73
"Blood Brother," 69–71
"Blood of the Dragon"
  "Part 1," 132–133
  "Part 2," 133–135
Booke, Sorrell, 109
Bossick, Bernard B., 143, 146
Bradbury, Lane, 71, 72
Brandt, Victor, 160
Brimley, A. Wilford, 142, 143
Brooks, Geraldine, 75
"Brothers Caine, The," 149–150
Brubaker, Tony, 128
"Brujo, The," 97–98
Burton, Wendell, 80
Busey, Gary, 90
Butler, Robert, 78, 83, 86, 90

Caine, Danny, 17, 68, 73, 83–84,
  126–127, 131, 149, 150–151
Caine, Henry, 68, 133, 134
Caine, Kwai Chang, 5, 12, 14, 24,
  26, 27–37, 64, 90, 122. See also
  Carradine, David; Young Caine
  (Grasshopper)
  and animal styles, 19–20
  background story of, 5–7
  casting of, 32–35
  character development of, 27–32,
    66–67
  in first-season episodes, 65–91
  in flashbacks, 16–17, 31
  flute of, 26, 48, 105
  grandson of, 163, 165–166
  great-grandson of, 160
  in Kung Fu: The Legend Contin-
    ues, 167
  in Kung Fu: The Movie, 154–157
  in Kung Fu: The Next Generation,
    160, 161
  in Kung Fu: The Pilot, 58–60
  and Master Po's death, 59–60
  in pebble scene, 97
  and props, 48
  in second-season episodes, 93–123
  son of, 156–157
  spiritual education of, 7, 9, 10–11,
    21–25
  and story development, 14, 16

and wardrobe changes, 51–53
Caine, Peter, 165–167
Caine, Richard, 106
Cameron, Michael, 75
Canary, David, 106
Carey, Timothy, 147
Carradine, Bruce, 108, 142, 143
Carradine, Calista, 172
Carradine, David, 12, 24, 26, 32,
  38, 60, 61, 64, 68, 79, 82, 90,
  124, 153, 157. See also Caine,
  Kwai Chang; Young Caine
  (Grasshopper)
  biography, 171–172
  on branding, 25
  on Caine's character, 30–31
  as director, 135, 136, 138–140
  Emmy nomination, 184
  as grandson of Caine, 163, 166
  on initial response to Kung Fu, 15
  in Kung Fu: The Movie, 155–156,
    157
  on Kung Fu story, 4–5, 7–8, 19, 21–
    22, 23
  on masters, 40, 42
  on second-season episodes, 94, 99
  on style of show, 9
  on third-season episodes, 127, 129,
    151
Carradine, Free, 172
Carradine, John, 67, 68, 69, 118,
  147, 148
Carradine, Kansas, 172
Carradine, Keith, 32, 35, 60, 83
Carradine, Robert, 67, 68, 69
"Cenotaph, The"
  "Part 1," 119–120
  "Part 2," 121–123
"Chains," 83–85, 184
"Chalice, The," 96–97
Chan, Kim, 167
Chant, David, 167
Chao, Harvey, 167
Charleson, Leslie Ann, 142
Chen, Tina, 77
Chow, David, 24, 33, 52, 60
  biography, 178–179
  on fighting, 49
Christie, Marcia, 161

Clark, Matt, 106
Clements, Calvin, Jr., 103
Colby, Barbara, 118
Colman, Booth, 99
Conklin, Mark W., 167
Contreras, Roberto, 141
Cooke, John C., 161
Coon, Gene L., 83
Cooper, Ben, 121
Cordero, Maria Elena, 97
Crane, Barry, 130, 145
Crays, Durrell Royce, 154
"Crossties," 113–115
Cruz, Brandon, 64, 65, 67
"Cry of the Night Beast," 125–
    126

Dales, Arthur, 99
Dandridge, Frank, 112
Daniels, Marc, 137, 142, 148,
    150
Dano, Royal, 75
"Dark Angel," 67–68
Darlow, David, 158, 160
Darrow, Henry, 97
da Silva, Howard, 104
Dawson, Juno, 112
De Meo, Paul, 158
"Demon God, The," 135–136
Dennis, John, 103
de Vargas, Vad, 149
"Devil's Champion, The," 136–
    137
Dheigh, Khigh, 81, 99, 138, 140
DiCenzo, George, 130
Dierkop, Charles, 96
Dillon, Oscar, 161
Dirkson, Douglas, 103
Doniger, Walter, 77, 98, 106
Donley, Robert, 118
Donner, Robert, 77
Doucette, John, 73
Douglas, Diana, 102
Douglas, Diane, 167
"Dream Within a Dream, A," 109–
    110
Dubbins, Don, 85
Dubin, Charles, 80, 85, 88
Duff, Howard, 109, 127

Dugan, John T., 98, 109, 115, 126,
    132, 147
Duggan, Andrew, 77
Dunlop, William, 167
Duran, Richard, 161

Eccles, Aimee, 78
Edwards, Paul, 83
Eisenmann, Ike, 87
Elam, Jack, 99
Elcar, Dana, 75, 95
"Elixir, The," 106
"Empty Pages of a Dead Book,"
    108–109
Esformes, Nate, 108
Everett, Mark, 161
"Eye for an Eye, An," 71–72, 73,
    184

Fairchild, Margaret, 103
Farber, Arlene, 112
Feinberg, Ronald, 78
Feliciano, Jose, 145, 146
Fernandez, Emilio, 97
Ferrer, Miguel, 160
Field, Gustave, 130
Fimple, Dennis, 113
Firestone, Eddie, 99
Flanders, Ed, 101
Fleming, Rhonda, 147
Fletcher, Bill, 80
"Flight to Orion," 149
Flores, Von, 167
Flynn, Neil, 161
Fong, Benson, 43, 60, 61, 69, 97,
    130
    biography, 176
Fong, Brian, 138, 140
Fong, Frances, 142
Fontanna, Dorothy C., 145
"Forbidden Kingdom, The," 146
Ford, Harrison, 113
Forsythe, Rosemary, 128, 129
Foster, Jodie, 81, 82
Fowley, Douglas V., 95
Foxworth, Robert, 108
Francis, Anne, 112
Francis, Ivor, 115
Frand, Harvey, 15–16

Frand, Harvey (*cont.*)
  on David Carradine, 32, 35
  on Keye and Ahn, 40–41
  on Pera, 36
  on sets, 47
French, Victor, 90
Friedlander, Howard, 4, 7, 57, 61
  biography, 180
  development of *Kung Fu*, 13–15
Fudge, Alan, 107
Fujioka, John, 136, 143
"Full Circle," 150–151
Furia, John, Jr., 61, 71, 73
  biography, 182
  on Caine's character, 30, 32
  on episodes, 94
  on film techniques, 49–50
  on flashbacks, 16–17, 32
  on pebble scene, 22
  on Pera, 36
  on popularity of *Kung Fu*, 8
  on violence, 10–11

Gackle, Kathleen, 69
*Gambler Four: The Luck of the
  Draw*, 153
Gammon, James, 118
Garland, Beverly, 145
"Garments of Rage, The," 137–
  138
Geer, Ellen, 157
Geer, Will, 90
Gehring, Ted, 110, 148–150
George, Chief Dan, 89–91
George, Lynda Day, 111
Gibson, Lary H., 143, 146
Gierasch, Stefan, 119, 120, 121
Gilles, Michael, 161
Glass, Spooner, 94
Glover, William, 95
Grasshopper. *See* Young Caine
  (Grasshopper)
Greene, Michael, 83, 84, 135
  biography, 178
  Emmy nomination, 184
  flutes of, 48
  on popularity of *Kung Fu*, 8
Griffith, James, 67
Gulager, Clu, 69

"Gunman, The," 106–107
Gunn, Moses, 87

Hagen, Ross, 75
Haid, Charles, 147
Hallier, Lori, 167
Harper, Paul, 67, 112
Harper, Robert, 157
Harris, Harry, 127, 130, 141, 143,
  149
Harushi, 143
Hatch, Richard Lawrence, 78
Healey, Myron, 103
Henteloff, Alex, 125
Hessler, Gordon, 146, 147
Heyman, Aaron, 161
Hill, Mariana, 115
Hingle, Pat, 73
Ho Chow, 167
Hole, Jonathan, 130
Holman, Rex, 99
Hong, James, 33, 43, 44, 46, 60, 61,
  99, 100, 117, 127, 128, 137, 143
  biography, 174
  on guest-starring, 1
  on makeup, 50–51
  on popularity of *Kung Fu*, 8
  on sets, 47
"Hoots, The," 104–106
Horino, Tad, 102, 135, 144
Howard, Rance, 104
Howell, Hoke, 147
Hoyos, Rudolfo, 97
Hubley, Season, 132
Huddleston, David, 101, 142
Hylands, Scott, 69

"In Uncertain Bondage," 111–112
Ito, Robert, 32, 60, 61, 95–96, 110
  biography, 177
  on ninja, 95–96

Jagger, Dean, 67
Jensen, Gail, 172
Jenson, Roy, 85
Joe, Jeanne, 144
Johnson, Arch, 115
Johnson, Don, 99
Johnson, George Clayton, 135

Jones, L. Q., 71, 147
Jory, Victory, 125
Jubinville, Kevin, 167

Kam Yuen, 24, 25, 69
  biography, 179
  on fighting, 49
  on makeup, 50
  on wardrobe, 51
Kan, Master, 5, 18, 22, 38. *See also*
  Ahn, Philip
  and animal styles, 19–20, 21
  character of, 39–40
  in first-season episodes, 66, 68, 70,
    71, 74, 75, 78, 81, 83
  in *Kung Fu: The Movie*, 155
  in pebble scene, 4, 58
  in second-season episodes, 97,
    104, 105, 108–109, 110, 111,
    112
  in third-season episodes, 128, 134–
    135, 136, 139–141
  wardrobe of, 51
Karpf, Elinor, 148–150
Karpf, Stephen, 148–150
Katkov, Norman, 143, 147
Keach, James, 95
Keane, Kerrie, 157
Keefer, Don, 149
Kelley, Paula, 160
Kelley, William, 81, 96, 119, 121,
  138, 140
Kelton, Richard, 126
Kenyon, Sandy, 107
Kim, Evan, 146
"King of the Mountain," 65–67
Knight, Don, 80
Korn, David Michael, 110, 135,
  138, 140
Kung Fu, (original TV pilot), 5, 6–7,
  57–60
  credits, 57–58, 60
  Emmy nominations, 184
  synopsis, 58–60
Kung Fu: The Legend Continues,
  163–167
  credits, 163, 167
Kung Fu: The Movie, 154–157
  credits, 156, 157

Kung Fu: The Next Generation,
  157–161
  credits, 157–158, 160
Kung Fu: The Return of Caine,
  153
*Kung Fu: The Way of the Tiger,
  The Sign of the Dragon*, 5
Kusatsu, Clyde, 132, 146
Kushida, Beverly, 95
Kuter, Kay E., 147
Kwan, Nancy, 119, 121, 122

"Lamb to the Slaughter, A," 141–
  142
Landau, Martin, 157
Lang, Doreen, 108
Lang, Richard, 73, 95, 97, 101, 103,
  106, 109, 111, 113, 117, 119, 121,
  128, 132, 154
  on third-season episodes, 126
  on visual elements, 9
Lansing, Robert, 167
"Last Raid, The," 94, 147
Lawrence, Carol, 126
Lee, Brandon, 155, 157, 158, 160,
  162
Lee, Bruce, 32, 157
Lee, Guy, 42–44
  biography, 179
Lee, Pat, 43
Leong, Dalton, 117
Leslie, Bethel, 115
Lew, Jocelyne, 117
Lewin, Richard, 79, 88
Lewis, Geoffrey, 83
Lewis, Robert M., 118
Li, Bernadette, 167
Liu, Frank Michael, 69, 130, 136,
  150
Locke, Sondra, 127
Loo, Richard, 60, 61, 67, 69, 71,
  102, 117, 136, 176
Louise, Tina, 109
Lucking, Bill, 87
Luke, Keye, 3, 20, 38, 43, 60, 61,
  157. *See also* Po, Master
  biography, 172
  and makeup, 51
  personality of, 40–42

Lupton, John, 148
Lynch, Ken, 65

Mabe, Byron, 81, 142
McCarthy, Nobu, 95
McDaniel, Charles A., 108
McIntire, Tim, 71, 93, 148, 150
Mack, Eddie, 161
McKinnon, Jason, 104
Macleod, Murray, 80
Mahoney, Jock, 104
Mako, 43, 77, 157
 biography, 175
Man, Margaret, 167
Manley, Stephen, 141, 142
Marden, Adrienne, 67
Maross, Joe, 145
Martin, Kiel, 87
Martinez, A, 126, 150
Master Kan. See Kan, Master
Master Po. See Po, Master
Matheson, Tim, 103
Matsusaka, Tom, 167
Maunder, Wayne, 60
Meadow, Herb, 75
Medina, Julio, 141
Megowan, Don, 106
Melzer, Barbara, 117
Menken, John, 130
Mercer, Mae, 93, 147
Merrill, Gary, 110
Michaelian, Katharyn, 97, 117, 127, 136
Michaelian, Michael, 97, 117, 127, 136
Middleton, Robert, 115
Millan, Victor, 96
Miller, Herman, 16, 27, 28, 61, 65, 67, 68, 69, 137, 181
Miller, Mark, 109
Mims, Bill, 81, 147
Moessinger, David, 85
Moore, Joanna, 150
Moreau, Nathaniel, 164, 167
Morita, Pat, 147
Mosely, Roger, 111
Moxey, John Llewellyn, 99, 108, 112, 115
Muldaur, Diana, 106

Muntner, Simon, 143
Murdock, Kermit, 69
"My Brother, My Executioner," 126–127

Naranjo, Ivan, 119, 121
Nardini, Tom, 130
Narita, Richard, 138, 140
"Nature of Evil, The," 118
Neal, Patricia, 132
Nelson, Ed, 88
Nettleton, Lois, 148
Newin, Robert, 106
Nielsen, Leslie, 148–150
"Night of the Owls, Day of the Doves," 112–113
"Nine Lives," 75–76
Nono, Claire, 112, 143
North, Sheree, 88
Novak, Shelly, 73, 118
Nuyen, France, 128

O'Brien, Kenneth, 125
Oh, Soon–Teck, 43, 61, 78, 114, 115, 116, 136
 biography, 175
Okazaki, Bob, 146
Olsen, Merlin, 75
Olson, James, 137
"One Step into Darkness," 142–143

Pace, Judy, 111
Page, Harrison, 137
Parfrey, Woodrow, 85
Parker, Lara, 65, 67
"Passion of Chen Yi, The" 114, 115–116
Pataki, Michael, 119, 121
Paul, Lee, 96
Pera, Radames, 2, 31, 60, 61, 82, 129. See also Young Caine (Grasshopper)
 biography, 173–174
 on "Grasshopper" nickname, 21–22
 and Kung Fu: The Movie, 156
 on makeup, 50
 on masters, 39, 41–42
 and pebble scene, 22–23
 on popularity of Kung Fu, 7
 and rice paper scene, 23–24

selected for role, 36–37
on set, 47
in third-season episodes, 135
Peters, Kelly Jean, 87
Philips, Lee, 110
Phillips, Robert, 130
Pickens, Slim, 108
Polsky, Abe, 111, 125
Po, Master, 38. *See also* Luke, Keye
 and ambition, 5–6, 30
 character of, 39–40
 death of, 5–6, 30, 48, 59–60
 in first-season episodes, 67, 76, 79,
  81, 85
 in grasshopper scene, 3
 in *Kung Fu: The Movie*, 156
 and makeup, 51
 in second-season episodes, 95, 96,
  97, 98, 118
 in third-season episodes, 131, 132,
  139, 142, 143, 146, 148
Poon, Alice, 167
Potter, Chris, 165, 167
Powers, Stephanie, 125
Prange, Laurie, 104
"Praying Mantis Kills, A," 79–81
"Predators, The," 130
Price, Eugene, 128
Prine, Andy, 107
Pyle, Denver, 90, 113

Quade, John, 127
Quo, Beulah, 43, 61, 126, 143
 biography, 174–175

Racimo, Victoria, 136
"Raiders, The." *See* "Way of Vio-
 lence Has No Mind, The"
Rainey, Ford, 85
Ramsey, Logan, 99
Reeves, James Lee, 101
Reisman, Del, 101
Reisner, Allen, 75
Renteria, Joe, 127
Rey, Alejandro, 141
Richards, Lloyd, 130
Ridgley, Robert, 119, 121
Riley, Jack, 107
Riley, Skip, 103

Robinson, Andy, 113
Roland, Gilbert, 96
Roman, Ruth, 109
Romero, Carlos, 108
Romero, Ned, 119, 121, 149
Rudd, Paul, 157
Ryusaki, Bill, 78

Sadoff, Fred, 85
Saito, Bill, 130, 144
"Salamander, The," 101–102
Salmi, Albert, 60, 75, 125
Sanford, Gerald, 118, 142
Saturday Night Live, 153–154
Saxton, John, 65
Seagull, Barbara (Barbara Hershey),
 138, 140
Schaffel, Marla, 167
Schallert, William, 80
Schlitt, Robert, 102–103, 113, 114–
 115
Serna, Pepe, 96
Shatner, William, 128, 129
Sherman, Robert, 142
Shibuya, Kinjo, 102, 128
Shigeta, James, 137, 146
Shimoda, Yuki, 117, 138, 140
Siegel, Lionel E., 104
Sierra, Gregory, 87
"Small Beheading, A," 124, 128–129
Smith, Denise Lee, 78
Smith, William, 96
Soble, Ron, 110
"Soldier, The," 103–104
Sololoff, Harvey, 167
Soto, Rosana, 99
"Soul Is the Warrior, The," 73–75
Specht, Robert, 141
Spell, George, 93
Spielman, Ed, 57, 61, 154, 158, 163
 biography, 180
 on Caine's character, 29–30
 and development of *Kung Fu*, 13–
  15, 17
 on Master Po, 40
 on popularity of *Kung Fu*, 4, 7
 on rice paper scene, 25
 on violence, 11
"Spirit Helper, The," 98–99

Spradlin, G. D., 90
"Squaw Man, The," 99–101
Sterling, Jan, 127
"Stone, The," 86–88
Street, Elliott, 99
Stroud, Don, 125
Stuart, Barbara, 88
Sullivan, Barry, 60, 113
"Sun and Cloud Shadow," 78–79
"Superstition," 85–86
Swofford, Ken, 112, 127

Tanner, Clay, 126
Tessier, Robert, 135
"Thief of Chendo, The," 143–144
"Third Man, The," 88–89
Thordsen, Kelly, 118
Thorpe, Jerry, 16, 32, 58, 61, 65, 67,
    69, 71, 73, 93, 95–96, 126
  biography, 181
  Emmy Award and nominations,
    184, 185
  on pebble scene, 23
  on style, 9
  on visual effects, 49
  on wardrobe, 51
"Tide, The," 77–78
Tobey, Ken, 81
Tochi, Brian, 135
Tong, Allan, 167
"Tong, The," 102–103
Totten, Robert, 102, 104
Townes, Harry, 71
Traylor, William, 110
Trueman, Matt, 167
Turich, Felipe, 97
Tyner, Charles, 81

Ullman, Daniel, 94
Urich, Robert, 69, 71

"Valley of Terror, The," 127–128
Vanders, Warren, 83, 111
"Vanishing Image, The," 130–132,
    185
Venus, Brenda, 135
Vernon, John, 126, 150

Wainwright, James, 126
Walsh, Edward, 117
Walter, Michael, 161
Waters, Ed, 61, 85, 111, 112, 125,
    137, 138, 140
Watson, Mills, 65
"Way of Violence Has No Mind,
    The," 110–111, 187
Weathers, Carl, 150
Weaver, Fritz, 110
"Well, The" 93–94
Wells, Halsted, 78
Westmore, Frank, 50, 184
Wharmby, Tony, 158
Whiteman, Frank, 103
Williams, Hal, 93, 147
Wingreen, Jason, 80
Wong, Carey, 102
Woodville, Katharine, 107
Woodward, Morgan, 78, 118
Woolf, Jack, 73, 184

Yniguez, Richard, 141
Yoshioka, Adele, 146
Young Caine (Grasshopper), 2. See
    also Caine, Kwai Chang; Pera,
    Radames
  character development of, 27–32
  in first-season episodes, 71, 74, 76,
    78, 80
  masters and, 39–40
  in pebble scene, 4, 22–23, 58
  Pera selected for role of, 35–36
  puzzlement of, 31–32
  in rice paper scene, 23–25, 26
  in second-season episodes, 98,
    104, 108–112, 117, 118
  and significance of "Grasshopper"
    nickname, 3, 21–22
  in third-season episodes, 128, 131,
    135, 146
Yung, Victor–Sen, 43, 60, 61, 80,
    99, 110, 135, 138, 140
  biography, 177

Zerbe, Anthony, 104, 130
Zweiback, A. Martin, 77, 86, 90, 106

Illustration Credits

ABOUT THE AUTHOR

Herbie J Pilato is an author, actor, singer, and songwriter. He was graduated from Nazareth College of Rochester, New York, in 1983, with a bachelor's degree in theater arts, and studied television and film at UCLA.

As a television actor, Pilato has appeared on *The Golden Girls*, *The Bold and the Beautiful*, *General Hospital*, and *Highway to Heaven*, among other shows. During his years as an NBC page, Pilato worked as a production liaison on several other TV shows, including *An All Star Salute to President "Dutch" Reagan*, *The Tonight Show*, and *Wheel of Fortune*.

Pilato is also the author of *The Bewitched Book: The Cosmic Companion to TV's Most Magical Supernatural Situation Comedy* (New York: Dell, 1992). In his lectures at local schools, colleges, and community organizations, Pilato uses his book to address issues of prejudice and self-esteem. Pilato also teaches at Writers and Books in upstate New York.